T0316585

Economic Development in Ghana and Malaysia

Economic Development in Ghana and Malaysia investigates why two countries that appeared to be at more or less the same stage of economic development at one point in time have diverged so substantially.

At the time of their independence from the UK in 1957, both Ghana and Malaysia were at roughly the same stage of economic development; in fact, Ghana's real per capita income was slightly ahead of Malaysia's. Since then, Ghana's development has been sluggish, while Malaysia's economy has taken off into sustained growth and today, the real per capita income of Malaysia is about five times that of Ghana. This volume examines the pre-colonial and colonial economies of both countries, and the economic policies pursued after independence. In doing so, it aims to identify policies which might have contributed to Malaysia's development and those which might have slowed Ghana's. The authors ask whether lessons can be learned from the successes of countries such as Malaysia.

This detailed comparative analysis will be useful to students and researchers of development economics as well as public policy makers in developing countries. It is written in language which makes it accessible to the general reader.

Samuel K. Andoh is Professor of Economics and currently the Director of the MBA Program at Southern Connecticut State University in New Haven, Connecticut, USA. In the past he served as Chair of the Economics and Finance Department and also as Dean of the School of Business. He spent a semester as a Senior Fulbright Scholar in Azerbaijan.

Bernice J. deGannes Scott is Associate Professor at the Economics Department, Spelman College, Georgia, USA.

Grace Ofori-Abebrese is Senior Lecturer at the Department of Economics, Kwame Nkrumah University of Science and Technology, Kumasi, Ghana.

Routledge Explorations in Development Studies

This Development Studies series features innovative and original research at the regional and global scale. It promotes interdisciplinary scholarly works drawing on a wide spectrum of subject areas, in particular politics, health, economics, rural and urban studies, sociology, environment, anthropology, and conflict studies.

Topics of particular interest are globalization; emerging powers; children and youth; cities; education; media and communication; technology development; and climate change.

In terms of theory and method, rather than basing itself on any orthodoxy, the series draws broadly on the tool kit of the social sciences in general, emphasizing comparison, the analysis of the structure and processes, and the application of qualitative and quantitative methods.

Practices of Citizenship in East Africa
Perspectives from Philosophical Pragmatism
Edited by Katariina Holma and Tiina Kontinen

Political Financing in Developing Countries
A Case from Ghana
Joseph Luna

Dilemmas of Regional and Local Development
Edited by Jerzy Bański

Security, Development and Violence in Afghanistan
Everyday Stories of Intervention
Althea-Maria Rivas

Economic Development in Ghana and Malaysia
A Comparative Analysis
Samuel K. Andoh, Bernice J. deGannes Scott and Grace Ofori-Abebrese

For more information about this series, please visit: www.routledge.com

Economic Development in Ghana and Malaysia

A Comparative Analysis

Samuel K. Andoh, Bernice J. deGannes Scott and Grace Ofori-Abebrese

Routledge
Taylor & Francis Group

LONDON AND NEW YORK

First published 2020 by Routledge

2 Park Square, Milton Park, Abingdon, Oxon OX14 4RN

605 Third Avenue, New York, NY 10017

Routledge is an imprint of the Taylor & Francis Group, an informa business

First issued in paperback 2021

British Library Cataloguing-in-Publication Data
A catalogue record for this book is available from the British Library

Library of Congress Cataloging-in-Publication Data
Names: Andoh, Samuel K. (Samuel Kojo), 1952– author. | deGannes
    Scott, Bernice J., author. | Ofori-Abebrese, Grace, author.
Title: Economic development in Ghana and Malaysia : a comparative
    analysis / Samuel K. Andoh, Bernice J. deGannes Scott, Grace
    Ofori-Abebrese.
Description: 1 Edition. | New York : Routledge, 2020. | Series: Routledge
    explorations in development studies | Includes bibliographical
    references and index.
Identifiers: LCCN 2019056581 (print) | LCCN 2019056582 (ebook) |
    ISBN 9781138486003 (hardback) | ISBN 9781351047289 (ebook)
Subjects: LCSH: Economic development—Ghana. | Economic
    development—Malaysia. | Ghana—Economic policy—21st century. |
    Malaysia—Economic policy—21st century. | Ghana—Politics and
    government—21st century. | Malaysia—Politics and government—
    21st century.
Classification: LCC HC1060 .A594 2020 (print) | LCC HC1060 (ebook) |
    DDC 338.9595—dc23
LC record available at https://lccn.loc.gov/2019056581
LC ebook record available at https://lccn.loc.gov/2019056582

ISBN: 978-1-138-48600-3 (hbk)
ISBN: 978-1-03-217496-9 (pbk)
DOI: 10.4324/9781351047289

Typeset in Times New Roman
by Apex CoVantage, LLC

This is to all the Andohs, especially my wife, Sharon, who allowed me to go to work on Fridays even though I had solemnly promised that I would be home to help babysit grandson Eli Kwame Andoh (I will make it up to the both of you).

To the children, Samuel K. Jr., Elizabeth Erica, and Rachel Abena and the grandchildren, Grace, Eli, Charlotte, and Caleb.

Contents

Figures

Tables

Preface

Writing any book is an arduous task, especially one that tries to explain why one country is developed and the other is not. The paths countries take to develop may broadly be the same but they are not exactly alike. Yet, if you grew up in Ghana in the 1960s, as I did, and have traveled to other countries (rich and poor) or read or about them, you cannot but wonder why Ghana, with its abundant natural resources and capable men and women, should be a poor country. The one country which people often compare to Ghana is Malaysia. Malaysia is in the tropics, just like Ghana. Malaysia is well endowed with natural resources, just like Ghana. Malaysia had the same colonial legacy as Ghana and became independent in the same year as Ghana, in 1957. At the time of independence, it was thought that Ghana had a better chance of making it than Malaysia. At that time, Ghana's income per person was slightly higher than that of Malaysia. Some 60 years later, Malaysia's income per person is about five times that of Ghana. Although many articles have been written about the subject, most do not offer sufficient details to thoroughly explain the disparity in economic performance between the two countries.

In this book we attempt to explain the causes of the disparity in growth between Ghana and Malaysia, and we speculate on whether Ghana could have done better. In looking at the data and the policies pursued by both countries over the past 60 or more years, one cannot but think of a passage in John Dryden's *Absalom and Achitophel* and ask: Did Ghana let the lucky revolution of its economic fate glide away like wind, and has it been repenting its folly since? Fortunately, it is a wheel, and there could be a second impression, another bent, and it could be seized – but only if Ghana learns from its past through studies such as ours.

Acknowledgments

I would like to thank the Faculty Development Grants Office at Southern Connecticut State University and the Dean of the School of Business, Ellen Durnin, for giving me the funds to travel to Malaysia in the summer of 2018 as I was researching materials for the manuscript. I also acknowledge the help I received from the many graduate students who passed through my office over the years: Elizabeth Tabaka, Susan Scully, Joseph Amarante, Elizabeth Wager, Grace Collins-Hovey, and Ekaterina Vezhenkova.

Thanks also go to Maria Celina Alles-Gonzalez, my secretary, who held the office together while I sneaked a few hours here and there to write a page or two. Thanks to Marisol Lopez-Castro for providing technical expertise when needed. Thanks to my colleagues, Yilma Gebremariam and James Thorson, whose brains I had to pick so many times for one thing or the other.

Finally, thanks to my co-authors, Bernice Scott and Grace Ofori-Abebrese, for being patient.

All opinions and errors of interpretation are solely the authors and not the institutions we work for or anybody else's.

1 Introduction

The process of economic development is dynamic, not static; as such, an economy's development over time is not readily observed in real time but only after the process is over or has reached a certain critical point. This is the major reason why, in spite of the fact that many countries have gone through the process of economic development and are now called developed countries, there is as yet no one precise method for prescribing how a developing country can develop.

One way to understand a country's development is to look back in time, at defining turning points, and determine if some important markers can be isolated to explain them. This, in essence, is what W. W. Rostow (1960) tried to do in his *Stages of Economic Growth.* According to Rostow's thesis, countries go through five distinct stages: (1) traditional society; (2) preconditions for takeoff; (3) the takeoff; (4) the drive to maturity; and (5) the age of high mass consumption. Rostow tried to identify the stages by unique markers. Notwithstanding the painstaking efforts to document the necessary and sufficient conditions needed for each stage to usher in the next, the thesis yielded no practical universal laws of application; today, only economic historians refer to it in any meaningful way. Nonetheless, Rostow's method provides insight into how one might go about extracting useful lessons for what a country should avoid during economic development. Further, the analysis provides an instructive method to better understand the development process; it can be used directly to compare countries that have had similar characteristics and were at the same level of development at one point in time and began the conscious effort of developing their economies at more or less the same time. Such direct comparisons come very close to conducting an experiment – something economists cannot normally do.

Two such countries that readily come to mind for this kind of analysis are Ghana and Malaysia. Ghana became independent from the British on March 6, 1957. At that time, it was economically at about the same level of development (as measured by the real per capita income) as Malaysia, which gained independence (Merdeka, as the Malaysians call it) from the British on August 31 of the same year. In 2007, Joseph Stiglitz, in a speech commemorating the 50th anniversary of Malaysian independence, observed that at independence, Malaysia's gross domestic product (GDP), in purchasing power parity (PPP) terms, was "some 5% below that of Ghana". The International Bank for Reconstruction and Development (IBRD, 1957) estimated the per capita income in the Gold Coast at £50 for 1955, which is the equivalent of about US$2,599 today.[1] Sixty years later, in 2017, it was US$2,046, less than at independence.[2]

Data from the Penn World table 9.1 show that in 1957, the Malaysian real GDP of US$18,808.31 million was slightly larger than that of Ghana, which was US$16,025.55 million. Ghana's real GDP per capita of US$2,640.56, however, exceeded that of Malaysia, which was then US$2,521.89.[3] Ghana's real GDP per capita continued to be higher than Malaysia's until 1965, when Malaysia's GDP per capita surpassed it. By then, the real GDP per capita of Malaysia had risen to US$3,164.86 and Ghana's was US$3,023.02. From 1955 to 1965, the real GDP of Malaysia grew at 5.54% a year; Ghana's grew at 5.27% – an insignificant difference. During the period, Malaysia's population grew even faster at 3.07% a year while Ghana's grew at 3.05%.

It should be borne in mind that increases in real GDP alone are not sufficient to improve welfare. Real GDP must grow faster than the rate at which population grows to increase the real per capita GDP. In Malaysia, real GDP grew at a faster pace than population; in Ghana, population increased faster than real GDP. Although the differences were not significant, it marked the beginning of a diversion which increased significantly by the 1970s. Both countries have exhibited fluctuations in population growth rates, as can be seen from Figure 1.1. While the correlation between population growth and income is clear, wealthier countries tend to have lower population growth rates, and the causality is less obvious. Is it the case that a lower population growth rate allows a country to become richer faster, or that the increase in income reduces the rate at which the population grows? Whatever the causality, many developing countries have adopted deliberate policies to control the rate at which their population grows. There is no doubt that the high population growth rate has diluted the gains from growth in Ghana, especially in recent times. Malaysia has been able to reduce the rate at which its population has grown, and as a result its GDP per capita has grown faster. Of course that is only a small part of the reason why Malaysia has grown faster than Ghana.

Malaysia's population growth rate reached a high of 3.26% in 1962, fluctuated over the succeeding 26 years, and began a steady decline after 1988 (but not without fluctuations that made it sometimes surpass that of Ghana). For the last 17 years, Malaysia's population growth rate has been

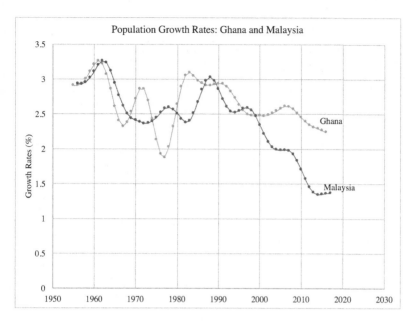

Figure 1.1 Population growth rates: Ghana and Malaysia
Source: www.rug.nl/ggdc/productivity/pwt/, accessed 7/2/2019.

below 2.0%. As of 2017, it stood at 1.37%, having been below 1.5% since 2012. Ghana's population growth rates have also exhibited the same fluctuations; reaching a high of 3.27% in 1962, the same year Malaysia recorded its highest. The growth rate has been decreasing, but not at the same rate as that of Malaysia. As of 2017, the population growth rate in Ghana was 2.25%, having decreased steadily from 2.61% in 2007. Not coincidentally, the slower population growth rate and the stability in the economy, among other factors, have allowed the Ghanaian economy to grow at an average rate of 4.16% between 2007 and 2017. Indeed, for Ghana, this growth rate represents the highest and the most extended sustained rate of growth of any previous period. At that rate, children born in 2017 should see the per capita real GDP double by the time they reach maturity. Interestingly, between 1957 and 2017, 4% is about the rate at which the Malaysian economy has grown annually, on the average (see Table 1.1 below).

The difference between the economy of Ghana and Malaysia today is dramatic when one considers where they both started. In 2014–2015, the poverty rate in Ghana was 24.2% of the population; it was 0.06% in Malaysia during the same year. In that same year, the gross national income (GNI)

Table 1.1 Real GDP/capita growth rate: 1957–2017

Period	Ghana	Malaysia
1957–1966	.06	2.63
1967–1976	−.98	6.04
1977–1986	−1.00	3.18
1987–1996	1.56	6.07
2007–2006	2.25	2.16
2007–2017	4.16	4.86
Average Growth	**1.01**	**4.16**

Source: Calculated from PWT 9.1 and UN population data.

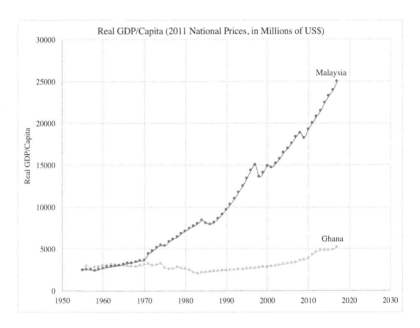

Figure 1.2 Real GDP/capita growth rates: Ghana and Malaysia
Source: www.rug.nl/ggdc/productivity/pwt/, accessed 7/2/2019.

per capita (Atlas method) in Ghana was US$1,590; in Malaysia, it was US$11,120 – nearly seven times greater. The life expectancy at birth in Ghana was 65.6 years; it was 75 years in Malaysia.[4] By just about any economic or social indicator, Malaysia is an upper-middle-income country; Ghana is a lower-middle-income country. Figure 1.2 shows the disparity in the growth rates of the two economies between 1957 and 2017, 60 years after independence.

In 1957, the Malaysian economy – with a real GDP of US$18,808.31 million – was 1.17 times larger than Ghana's economy, with a real GDP of US$16,025.55. Since Malaysia's real GDP per capital exceeded that of Ghana in 1965, there was a steady widening gap between the two countries, reaching its highest in 1997 when the ratio of Malaysia's real GDP to that of Ghana was 6.69 and the real GDP per capita of Malaysia was US$15,010.45 and Ghana's was US$2,701.73 (a difference of about five and a half times).

In the 60 years between 1957 and 2017, Malaysia's real GDP has grown at an average annual rate of 6.37% while its population has grown at 2.43%. Ghana's real GDP has grown at 3.99% a year, but its population has grown at 2.66%. The greater real GDP growth rate in Malaysia, coupled with a lower population growth rate over the same period, compared with the lower real GDP growth rate and a faster population growth rate in Ghana meant that Malaysia's real GDP per capita was getting increasingly larger compared to Ghana, but it also meant that Ghana's real GDP per capita was declining. The gap between the two countries was widening, not closing. Table 1.2 summarizes the discussion.

When one looks at the data by decades, there is only one decade (1997–2006) when real GDP per capita grew faster in Ghana than it did in Malaysia (see Table 1.3).

Table 1.2 Population and GDP per capita growth rates

Country	Growth Rates			Real GDP/Capita Years to Double
	Real GDP	*Population*	*Per Capita*	
Malaysia	6.37	2.43	3.94	18
Ghana	3.99	2.66	1.33	54

Source: PWT 9.1, UN population estimates, authors' calculations.

Table 1.3 Decennial growth rates

Decade	Real GDP/Capita Growth Rate	
	Ghana	*Malaysia*
1957–1966	.06	2.63
1967–1976	−.98	6.04
1977–1986	−1.00	3.18
1987–1996	1.56	6.07
1997–2006	2.25	2.16
2006–2016	4.16	4.86

Source: PWT9.1, www.rug.nl/ggdc/productivity/pwt/, accessed 7/2/2019.

If one places the endpoint of the comparison period at 2007, the picture gets worse. From 1957 to 2007, the real GDP of Ghana grew at a paltry 0.57% while Malaysia's grew at 4.13%.

Ghana and Malaysia

No two countries are indeed exactly alike, but sometimes there are enough similarities between them to make comparisons inevitable. Not only did Malaysia and Ghana go through the same colonial experience and inherit similar colonial legacies at the time of their independence in 1957, but both countries were also more or less at the same level of economic development. Their per capita GDPs did not differ much, and the structures of the economies were alike in many respects. They were both mostly dependent on the export of a few primary products: tin and rubber for Malaysia; cocoa, gold and timber for Ghana. They both inherited the British parliamentary system of government as well as its educational system. Malaysia is about 1.4 times bigger than Ghana (it has a land area of 328,657 square kilometers compared to Ghana's 227,533 square kilometers). It also has a much longer coastline (4,657 kilometers along the peninsula jutting out of the mainland of Asia and 2,607 kilometers along the border with Indonesia). Its strategic location in the Strait of Malacca and in the South China Sea gives it a maritime advantage. Ghana has a coastal line of 539 kilometers along the Gulf of Guinea. While Malaysia is closer to the big Asian markets of China and Japan, Ghana is closer to the older big markets of the eastern United States and the UK.[5] Both countries are tropical, north of the equator, with Ghana at 8°N and Malaysia at 2°30′N.

Malaysia, like Ghana, is a multiethnic society. It has three main ethnic groups: The Malays, who make up about more than half the population; the Chinese, who comprise about 22%; and the Indians, who comprise 6.7%. There are other smaller minority groups, including the descendants of the Portuguese (the Eurasians). Similarly, Ghana has several ethnic groups. The largest, the Akans, occupy the middle part of the country down to the southwestern coastal areas and constitute about 47.5% of the population. The Mole-Dagbon, in the eastern part of the Northern Region, represent approximately 16.6% of the population, and the Ewes, in the east, bordering the Republic of Togo, comprise about 13.9% of the population.[6] According to the Pew Research Centre (Religion and Public Life), about 61% of the Malaysian population is Muslim, followed by Buddhism and Hinduism. The confluence of ethnicity, religion, economic power, and politics has been the root cause of Malaysia's conflicts, notably the May 1969 race riots and the October 1987 disturbances (see Jomo Kwame Sundaram (1988)). In

Ghana, about 71.2% of the people classify themselves as Christians, while 17.6% classify themselves as Muslims. Some have argued that in Ghana, these differences have manifested themselves in the multiplicity of military coup d'états, which have created instability over a long period (see Asante and Gyima-Boadi (2004)).

Snodgrass (1995) argues that Malaysia has far more structural resemblance to other developing countries of the world than it has with the northeast Asian countries (Taiwan, South Korea, Hong Kong, and Singapore) to which it is often compared. Indeed, Malaysia has much in common with other developing countries of the world, like Ghana. Both Malaysia and Ghana share a common colonial heritage as well as multiethnic and pluralistic religious societies. As resource-rich colonies of the British, the patterns of economic development during the colonial period were similar; the British, the colonial power, saw the colonies as places to extract resources to feed their industries. This behavior is not different from how colonial powers behaved everywhere they colonized, except in the places where they settled. The commonalities Ghana and Malaysia share are good reasons to use Malaysia as a comparator for Ghana when discussing a case study in economic development.

A preliminary look

There is no doubt that the decisions made in the very early days after independence determined the path the two economies would take later and how they would fare. A secret Special Memorandum issued by the US Central Intelligence Agency (CIA) in 1967, and authorized for release in 2003, noted that at the time of the 1966 coup d'état that overthrew the government of Ghana, the country had "squandered US$500 million foreign exchange reserves and ran up new foreign debts of some US$700 million on unsound projects".[7] For many people, this is the major reason cited for the failure of economic policies in Ghana post-independence. There is no doubt that there is some hyperbole in the statement. The expenditure of $1.2 billion in the space of some ten years or less can be certainly classified as "squandering". As will be discussed in later chapters, the reasons for the poor performance of the Ghanaian economy are more than the squandering of resources; it is *how* the resources were squandered. To begin with, the change in the orientation of the Ghanaian economy from a market-driven one to a state-planned socialist economy in the middle of the 1960s probably did more to dampen the potential of the economy than any single factor alone. It took about 20 years (into the mid-1980s) to attempt to re-orient the economy back to what it was, and perhaps another 20 years (into the 2000s) for it to get any sense of direction. By contrast, Malaysia, even when it introduced state enterprises, did so in a way that did not upset the already settled market orientation of the economy. An equally important factor that may have accounted for the poor growth in Ghana and the excellent growth in Malaysia is the fact that between 1966 and roughly 1998, Ghana was politically unstable. The country went through several coups d'état, attempted coups d'état and fear of coups d'état. Political instability breeds risk, real or perceived. Where there is risk, foreign investors demand a premium or simply avoid the country. This can be seen in the amount of foreign direct investment that flows into a country.

As Table 1.4 shows, net inflow of foreign direct investment (FDI) in Ghana was very low compared to Malaysia.[8]

FDI tends to flow to countries that are perceived to be stable and can offer steady, high rates of returns on investment. If one looks at Table 1.4, one cannot but conclude that the low net inflows of FDI up to 2005 must have been partially due to the instability in Ghana, and the high FDI rates in the 2000s due to the relative stability thereafter. By contrast, in Malaysia, in one form or the other, the same alliance or coalition of political parties has been running the government since independence and thus providing the assurance of stability. The result is a steady inflow of net FDI. Stability and continuity create a conducive environment for businesses, especially for countries dependent on the rest of the world for capital and technical knowledge for growth. Nothing could be more of a deterrent to foreign investment than instability; instability is synonymous with risk, and risk drives away capital. This is not to say that Malaysia has not had its own share of instability; the communist insurgency from roughly 1948 to 1990 (Kheng, 2009), the 1964 racial riots which led to Singapore exiting from the federation in 1965, and the racial riots of 1969 are all factors that could have derailed the path of the economy. Malaysia experienced some of the same problems Ghana did, but it managed to overcome them.

Table 1.4 Foreign direct investment, net inflows (% of GDP)

Period	Malaysia	Ghana
1976–1985	3.53	0.37
1986–1995	4.96	0.95
1996–2005	3.51	1.90
2006–2015	3.19	5.10

Source: World Development Indicators, https://data.worldbank.org/indicator/BX.KLT.DINV.WD.GD.ZS, accessed 7/5/2019.

Another explanatory factor is the rate at which both countries saved. As Table 1.5 shows, Malaysia has outperformed Ghana in every decade since 1966 in the percentage of GDP saved. Between 1966 and 1975, Malaysia saved 18.94% of its GDP compared to Ghana's 10.73%. After that, Ghana's savings rate fell while Malaysia's rose, reaching a high of 44.30% between 1996 and 2005. In that decade, Malaysia's savings, as a percentage of GDP, was 6.4 times that of Ghana (Column 4 in Table 1.5). The high domestic savings and the high FDI meant faster capital accumulation, greater capital per person, and thus higher output per person.

The real story would be how Malaysia was able to generate a high savings rate and attract the high net foreign direct investment. These are some of the actual practical lessons to be learned from Malaysia.

Stieglitz (2007) argues that Malaysia looked at the countries of South Korea, Taiwan, China, and Thailand and adopted a development strategy that emphasized a high savings rate and closing the knowledge gap in education and technology; minimizing ethnic tensions; adopting a free-market ideology; and being pragmatic. Being pragmatic meant doing whatever worked: creating state enterprises where they were needed, providing incentives to the private sector, and cooperating with the private sector when necessary. In doing so, Malaysia established new institutions to do things the state felt had to be done. Some of the institutions that were established have achieved success; these include the Federal Land Development Authority (FELDA, 1956); the Malaysian Investment Development Authority (MIDA, 1967); the Permodalan Nasional Berhad (PNB, 1978); and more recently, the Malaysian Digital Economy Corporation (MEDC, 1996). Similarly, Ghana established several state institutions to move its economy forward. Many of them did not achieve the impact the government had hoped for. The Ghana Cocoa Board (previously the Ghana Cocoa Marketing Board, established in 1947) probably did the best in promoting cocoa production by protecting farmers from world price volatility and raising substantial revenues for the government. One could also argue that the heavy taxes it imposed on farmers probably

Table 1.5 Gross domestic savings (% of GDP)

Period	Malaysia	Ghana	MYS/GHA
1966–1975	18.94	10.73	1.77
1976–1985	30.55	5.60	5.46
1986–1995	36.36	6.49	5.60
1996–2005	44.30	6.92	6.40
2006–2015	38.58	6.84	5.64

Source: World Development Indicators, https://data.worldbank.org/indicator, accessed 7/5/2019.

contributed to the decline in cocoa production and Ghana losing its position as the leading producer of cocoa in the world to the Ivory Coast.

Goal and objectives

Many Ghanaians and others see the rapid growth of the Malaysian economy and the stagnant state of the Ghanaian economy as the result of wrong policies pursued by the government of Ghana, and correct ones pursued by Malaysia. It is almost an axiom among educated Ghanaians that at the time of independence, Ghana and Malaysia were more or less on par economically. The evidence thus far seems to suggest so. Nobody disputes the fact that Malaysia is now some ten times more prosperous than Ghana. Yet, the question of why the huge disparity exists has not been satisfactorily explained beyond platitudes such as unsound state enterprises, squandering of reserves, political and diplomatic activities designed to further continental ambitions. The general goal of this book is to help understand why Ghana and Malaysia ended up, 60 years after independence, in such starkly different economic states. More specifically, the objectives are:

1   To identify the determinants of growth in both countries;
2   To identify and examine the specific policies pursued by Ghana and Malaysia immediately after independence and their short-term and long-term impacts on the economy;
3   To determine the extent to which the successful Malaysian policies could be duplicated in Ghana, or indeed elsewhere in Africa.

Economic development

Some development economists argue that in the early stages of development there is the need for a benevolent dictator.[9] The dictator need not be a strong man or woman but if they are, they must have the interest of the country at heart and possess enough power to compel people to do what they would normally not do in their own self-interest. The leader or leaders must be benevolent and must preside over a system that is *autocratically capitalistic*.[10] People who argue in this vein cite the countries of Taiwan, South Korea, Singapore, and in recent times, China. This argument runs counter to modern mainstream economic thought, which mostly argues for a more open society. Both Ghana and Malaysia began with a British colonial legacy that was similar in several respects: both had a parliamentary democratic system and a free market. It has been argued that Malaysia adopted an *autocratic capitalistic* model of development while Ghana, in the early 1960s, adopted an *autocratic command system*. Shortly after independence,

Ghana turned to a socialist model of development. The then prime minister, Kwame Nkrumah, in launching the Seven-Year Development Plan, indicated that it was the intention to have the country transformed completely "into a strong, industrialised socialist economy and society".[11] Therefore, as Ghana began to set up state-owned enterprises (SOEs) on the grounds that they would provide increasing and assured revenues to the state, Malaysia continued on the path of private enterprise, not disturbing the existing production systems, but mobilizing resources to ensure that additional growth would include the indigenous population.

Malaysia's economy used planning as a tool to enhance growth; *indicative planning*. Under this mode of planning, the state did not always own the means of production; instead, it made plans and offered inducements to steer the private sector in the direction it felt would be "best" for the economy to achieve the goals of the plan. While Ghana's economy was also planned, in 1963/1964, the government turned to *central planning*. The state not only made plans, but it also implemented them through the SOEs. The state acquired the means of production and made decisions on how best to use the resources it had acquired.

Malaysia, like Ghana, began life as a low-income agricultural economy, dependent almost entirely on the exports of tin and rubber – commodities which were then in high demand in the West for industry. Ghana, at the time, also depended almost entirely on the exports of primary commodities – mainly cocoa, timber, gold, and manganese. In other words, Ghana and Malaysia were similar in their dependence on primary commodities for exports and foreign exchange. Indeed, this was how most of the colonies were organized. They were valued as suppliers of raw materials for the colonial powers in Europe. In turn, they imported finished goods from Europe or wherever the colonial power deemed appropriate. The same was true of the United States during the period when it was a British colony up until the latter part of the 18th century. How did Malaysia shed its primal colonial economy to become an upper-middle-income economy?

Methodology

We combine two general methods for the study. We use comparative analysis to do a case study of Ghana and Malaysia. The case study method is replete in the economics literature, especially when it comes to economic growth and development. The methodology does not eschew the use of other tools to study specific issues. For example, Chow and Lin (2002) used comparative analysis to understand the disparity in growth in China and Taiwan, but that did not stop them from employing other tools. To understand why the savings rate in Malaysia is higher than that in Ghana, it may be necessary to employ some other tool to determine the factors that explain savings in both countries. The beauty of comparative analysis is that it tethers the authors to the issues of importance; namely, the disparity in the economic performance of the two countries: why Ghana and Malaysia are so markedly different when they appear to have started from the same level of economic development.

One must bear in mind that the disparity in economic performances of Ghana and Malaysia is due primarily to economic policies pursued or not pursued and the consequences thereof. Both countries pursued development planning and import substitution (see Cho (1990), Steel (1972)). One has succeeded, and one has not, or at least has not yet made the breakthrough. This is an interesting case study.

This book is not about politics but rather economic development and, one may argue, political economy. One cannot divorce economics from politics, especially when it comes to economic policy. The primary objective of this book is to examine the paths Malaysia and Ghana took to reach their current markedly different economic conditions. It is a case study in economic development, and it takes a heuristic approach to understand and educate policy makers, particularly in developing countries, who have the unenviable task of making decisions that will affect the lives of thousands of people now and in the future. To say that by reading this book, one would always be able to adopt the proper economic policy to speed economic development would be an exaggeration. Nonetheless, to know why, confronted with the same goal of economic development, one country chose a road which led to rapid development and the other a road which led to stagnation is important in understanding what course of action to take. (Economic development is easy to recognize once it has taken place. Its path or process is not, however, easy to predict. That is the reason why history can be so important. By studying two countries that appeared to have started from the same state in the past, we hope to shed some light on the unobserved process of development that took place over time.)

Organization of the book

This book does not cover the whole subject matter of economic development; rather, it is positioned as a supplementary reader for students in economic development and political economy, as well as policy makers, as a means for studying economic theories at work. As a supplementary reader, it can be used to demonstrate how some of the theories work specifically. It is organized as follows:

Chapter 2 discusses the economic policies pursued by the two countries in the period immediately before independence and after independence.

Chapter 3 reviews some of the major basic theories of economic growth, such as the Harrod-Domar and the Solow growth models. These will provide the theoretical background to bridge Chapter 2 and Chapters 4 and 5.

Chapter 4 reviews the literature on the determinants of economic growth in Ghana. There is a large volume of work detailing the factors that have inhibited and or enhanced growth in Ghana. The intention is to identify the significant factors that have contributed to Ghana's economic growth, or the lack of it.

Chapter 5 surveys the literature on the determinants of economic growth in Malaysia. As with Ghana, a lot has been written in an attempt to explain the fast growth of the Malaysian economy. Our intention is to review the literature and isolate the factors that may have contributed to the economy's performance.

Chapter 6 discusses and analyses the successes and failures of the policies pursued by the two countries and seeks to identify the factors that led to their divergent economic performances, provides a brief summary and draws some lessons from the discussions that we believe will be useful to policy makers and students of economic development and public policy.

General footnote

In this manuscript, we do not make any attempt to distinguish Malaysia as presently constituted, from its predecessor entities, namely *Malaya Union* (1946), now Peninsular Malaysia, the *Federation of Malaya* (1948), which comprised the two British Straits Settlements of Penang and Malacca, together with Johor, Kedah, Kelantan, Sembilan, Pahang, Perak, Perlis, Selangor, and Terengganu. In 1963, Sabah and Sarawak (Eastern Malaysia) and Singapore joined the Federation of Malaya to become *Malaysia*. Singapore left in 1965. The reason we do not make the distinction is that, since 1957, when the Federation of Malaya became independent, the nucleus of Malaysia has always been present. The period when Malaysia experienced the most rapid growth of interest in this manuscript does not include Singapore.

Notes

1 www.fx-exchange.com/gbp/usd-1955-exchange-rates.html, accessed 3/15/2019.
2 https://data.worldbank.org/indicator/NY.GDP.PCAP.CD?end=1960&locations=KR-GH-JP&start=1960&view=bar, accessed 3/15/2019.
3 www.rug.nl/ggdc/productivity/pwt/, accessed 7/2/2019.
4 http://data.worldbank.org/country, accessed 1/12/2016.

5 www.marinetraffic.com/en/voyage-planner, accessed 6/22/2017.
6 www.cia.gov/library/publications/the-world-factbook/geos/gh.html, accessed 6/22/2017.
7 Ghana's Political and Economic Malaise, July 19, 1967, Central Intelligence Agency, Board of National Estimates, Special Memorandum No. 5–67, Sherman Kent, Chairman.
8 Foreign direct investments are the net inflows of investment to acquire a lasting management interest (10% or more of voting stock) in an enterprise operating in an economy other than that of the investor. It is the sum of equity capital, reinvestment of earnings, other long-term capital, and short-term capital, as shown in the balance of payments. This series shows net inflows (new investment inflows less disinvestment) in the reporting economy from foreign investors and is divided by GDP. World Bank.
9 Gilson, Ronald J. and Curtis J. Milhaupt, "Economically Benevolent Dictators: Lessons for Developing Democracies", *Columbia Law and Economics Working Paper No. 371*, March 4, 2010.
10 See a 10/10/2010 post by Gary Becker on The Becker-Posner Blog, "Democracy or Autocracy: Which Is Better for Economic Growth?", www.becker-posner-blog.com/2010/10/democracy-or-autocracy-which-is-better-for-economic-growth-becker.ht, accessed 4/10/2017.
11 Foreword to *Seven-Year Plan for National Reconstruction and Development*, Financial Years 1963/4–1969/70, Office of the Planning Commission, Accra March 16, 1964.

Bibliography

Asante, Richard and E. Gyima-Boadi (2004). "Ethnic Structure, Inequality and Governance of the Public Sector in Ghana", Part of UNRISD *Project on Ethnic Structure, Inequality and Governance of the Public Sector*.

Cho, George (1990). *The Malaysian Economy Spatial Perspectives*, Abingdon, UK, Routledge.

Chow, Gregory and An-loh Lin (2002). "Accounting for Economic Growth in Taiwan and Mainland China: A Comparative Analysis", *Journal of Comparative Economics*, Vol. 30, No. 3, September, pp. 507–530.

Collier, Paul and Jan W. Gunning (1999). "Why Has Africa Grown Slowly", *Journal of Economic Perspectives*, Vol. 13, No. 3, Summer, pp. 3–22.

IBRD (1957). *Report of the Mission to the Gold Coast*, IBRD Department of Operations, Europe, Africa and Asia, February 4.

Kheng, Cheah Boon (2009). "The Communist Insurgency in Malaysia, 1948–1990: Contesting the Nation-State and Social Change", *New Zealand Journal of Asian Studies*, Vol. 11, No. 1, June, pp. 132–152.

Radelet, Steven and Jeffrey Sachs (1998). "Shipping Costs, Manufactured Exports, and Economic Growth", www.earth.columbia.edu/sitefiles/file/about/director/pubs/shipcost.pdf Accessed 7/5/2019.

Sachs, J.D. and Mark Warner (1997). "Sources of Slow Growth in African Economies", *Journal of African Economies*, Vol. 6, pp. 335–376.

Snodgrass, D.R. (1995). *Successful Economic Development in a Multi-Ethnic Society: The Malaysian Case* (No. 503). Harvard Institute for International Development, Harvard University.

Steel, William F. (1972). "Import Substitution and Excess Capacity in Ghana", *Oxford Economic Papers*, New Series, Vol. 24, No. 2, July, pp. 212–240.

Stieglitz, Joseph (2007). "The Malaysia Miracle", www.project-syndicate.org/commentary/the-malaysian-miracle#paragraphId=3b1f340346f86f702f203905 Accessed 7/5/2019.

Sundaram, Jomo Kwame (1988). "Malaysia: Economic Recession, Ethnic Relations and Political Freedom", *Cultural Survival Quarterly Magazine*, Vol. 12, No. 3, pp. 55–63.

Teik, Khoo Boo. "Ethnic Structure, Inequality and Governance in the Public Sector: Malaysian Experiences", Governance (2000–2009), Paper No: 20, Code: PP-DGHR-20, in Ethnic Structure, Inequality and Governance of the Public Sector.

2 Ghana and Malaysia
Pre- and post-colonial economic planning and policies

Introduction

Although the histories of both Ghana and Malaysia go back several hundreds or thousands of years before colonization, neither country existed as a single unified entity; instead, they comprised several autonomous kingdoms/chiefdoms (Ghana) or sultanates (Malaysia). In the Gold Coast, as Ghana was called before independence, the British initially controlled the coastal areas and traded with the interior territories from their forts and castles strewn along the coast, using the coastal tribes as intermediaries and buffers between them and the powerful Asante Kingdom to the north. After 1901, when the last of several skirmishes or wars between the Asantes and the British ended,[1] and "all Asante was declared a colony by conquest", (Wilks, 2004), the Colony (the coastal areas), the Asante Territory, and the Northern Territory were combined to become one unit. The Volta Region did not become a part of the Gold Coast until the plebiscite of 1956, which was when the present boundaries of Ghana came into existence. Similarly, Malaysia is the result of the merger of parts of British Malaya and British Borneo. The Sultanates of Malaysia were not unified until 1930; it took 60 more years and several treaties to do so. The territories of Sabah and Sarawak, which were separate British colonies, joined the Malaya Federation in 1963 along with Singapore. Malaysia, in its present form, dates back to 1965, after Singapore seceded. Currently, Malaysia consists of 13 states: Johor, Kedah, Kelantan, Melaka, Sembilan, Pahang, Perak, Perlis, Penang, Selangor, and Terengganu are all on Peninsular Malaysia; and Sabah and Sarawak are in Eastern Malaysia, separated from Peninsular Malaysia by the South China Sea. There are also three federal territories: Kuala Lumpur, Labuan, and Putrajaya.

In trying to explain the factors that caused Ghana and Malaysia to drift so significantly apart in growth and development, one has first to determine when the drift began and then to identify the economic policies initiated in the past that may have contributed to the later disparity between the countries. The effects of economic policies do not usually have an immediate impact on the economy; rather, the impacts may appear with a lag and may persist for a long period, declining slowly. To explain the present economic conditions, one must look back to the policies that were introduced in the past. For both Ghana and Malaysia, the past that this book considers includes the colonial period up to 1957 and the immediate post-colonial period, up to roughly the mid-2000s or before, when the two economies were no longer in the same income level classification: Malaysia became an upper-middle-income country and Ghana a lower-middle-income country (July 1, 2011).[2]

It should be noted that we are not trying to explain the performance of Malaysia's economy as such; rather, we are trying to understand the factors that helped the Malaysian economy outperform Ghana's over the period of roughly 1957 to 2007 and beyond.

In this chapter, we review economic policies during the colonial and immediate post-colonial periods as the first step in explaining the disparity in economic performance between Ghana and Malaysia.

Colonial and immediate post-colonial economic policies: Ghana

Both Ghana and Malaysia are tropical countries which are well endowed with natural resources. In the Gold Coast, initially, it was the alluvial gold, then timber and later trade in humans (abolished in 1814) which came to dominate trade with Europe. The Portuguese had suspicions that there were rich fertile lands from which gold and other goods flowed to North Africa. Although they were looking for a sea route to Asia, the thought of diverting the trans-Saharan gold route would not have been far from their minds. By 1482, the Portuguese had built their first castle in Elmina (in the Gold Coast); they were not the last colonizers. The Dutch, and then the French, the British, the Germans and the Scandinavians soon followed.[3] During these early years, economic activities revolved around trade in gold and ivory from the natives, in exchange for products such as metal artifacts (knives, etc.), rum and guns from the Europeans. Later, trade in slaves was to dominate. As many writers (including Sachs and Malaney, 2002) have observed, the malarial tropical environment was hostile to Europeans and may very well have inhibited large-scale European settlements in West Africa (as well as Malaysia), but it also dictated the nature of interactions with the natives and the type of economic structure that would prevail.

In the Gold Coast, European interaction with the natives was mostly with the coastal tribes. The coastal people acted as intermediaries between the colonizers and other tribes, transporting goods from the interior to the coast.

The Asantes, between the coast and the north, sought to control the trade routes, which led to frequent conflicts with the coastal tribes and ultimately the British. When the British took control of the colony, economic development projects they initiated were intended to make it easier for the extraction of resources from the interior region (gold, timber, manganese, etc.) – a pattern of development which was to persist for a long time and has not disappeared even today.

Very early in the 20th century, a rail line was constructed from the coast to the interior to facilitate the movement of the extracted raw materials. A newly introduced product, cacao (cocoa), became a major cash crop and gave a significant boost to the colonial economy. While the exports of gold, timber, diamonds, manganese, and minerals continued, cocoa became the major exported crop, replacing gold. After cocoa's introduction into the colony in the 1890s, production rose steadily, reaching a high of 572,000 long tons (about 38% of total world's output) in the 1964/1965 season, according to data from Gill and Duffus (1967). More importantly, the production of the crop spread to all the regions in the southern part of Ghana, involving a lot of workers because of the small-scale nature of farming. Many cocoa farmers became very wealthy, and the colony also benefited from this wealth. In 1955, external trade statistics showed that the colony exported £96 million worth of goods, and that cocoa accounted for £66 million or 69% of that, gold for 0.38%, timber 8.33%, diamonds 6.25%, and manganese 5.21%.[4] The colony was dependent on one major product for export earnings: it was a mono-crop economy. Nonetheless, the gross national product (GNP) was £235 million (US$658 million) and per capita income was £50 (US$140), which, when converted into 2019 figures, translates into a GNP of US$6,206.22 million and per capita income of US$1,320.47. This made the colony relatively wealthy.

Since no processing of the cocoa bean took place in the colony, the additional multiplier effect in employment and income that could have been generated never materialized. To a large extent, it still is the case today that raw materials are mainly exported. In 1949, only one long ton of cocoa was ground in the colony. Cocoa grinding reached a high of 51 long tons in 1966, at a time when Ghana was producing about 28% of total world output of the crop. In the same year, only 14% and 17% of the cocoa was exported as butter and powder, respectively. The less processing that takes place, the less value is added to the exported product. The same was true of just about all the other major exports. Timber, which at the very least could have been exported as sawn timber or lumber, was exported as logs. A large amount of bauxite is still exported in its natural state to be processed into aluminum elsewhere. Nevertheless, the exports of these primary commodities made the colony rich.

The structure of the economy was agrarian; employment data quoted by Szereszewski (1965) on the coastal cities show that the structure of the economy in the early years was not very different from what it must have been before colonization. In 1891, a Census of Selected Employment Occupations indicated that 62.5% of those employed were in fishery and farming, and 18.31% were classified as providing services (domestics, construction, blacksmiths, masons, butchers, carpenters, mechanics, goldsmiths, shoemakers, tailors, bakers, washermen, dressmakers, weavers, laborers, and painters). The structure of the economy had not changed much by 1960, according to Birmingham, Neustadt and Omaboe (1966, see Table 2.1).

Economic policy: planning and development in Ghana

The first development plan: Ghana 1920–1930

The economic structure of the colony did not experience any major shift until the 1920s, when deliberate efforts began to be made by the colonial government to develop the economy. Between 1920 and 2014, there are records of over 15 development plans for the development of the Gold Coast and Ghana. It is through these plans that one can discern the economic policies the various governments pursued over the years. The two most structurally transformative and well-remembered plans are the colonial Governor Guggisberg's Ten-Year Development Plan 1920–1930 and the post-independence Seven-Year Development Plan 1963/1964–1969/1970. Each plan's effects on the economy lasted for a long time.

Although neither plan lasted the entirety of the period envisioned by the planners, they both set in motion forces that moved the economy in the direction it was go for several decades after they were launched and abandoned. For this reason, these two have also left indelible, visible marks on the economy and have been seared into the collective memories of many Ghanaians.

Table 2.1 Employment: main sectors of Ghana's economy, 1960

Sector	Numbers	Percent
Agriculture, Forestry, Hunting and Fishing	1,578,880	61.65
Mining and Quarrying	48,430	1.89
Manufacturing	235,240	9.19
Construction	89,370	3.49
Electricity, Gas, Water and Sanitary Services	14,110	0.55
Commerce	371,500	14.51
Transportation and Communication	68,420	2.67
Service	155,090	6.06
TOTAL	**2,561,040**	**100**

The first serious attempt at a comprehensive economic development plan for the Gold Coast colony took place under Gordon Guggisberg, governor from 1919 to 1927. He had worked in the Gold Coast as a surveyor prior to being appointed a governor and therefore knew the terrain very well. The Ten Year Development Plan 1920–1930 he proposed was seen then, and now, as structurally transformational. It was intended to lay the foundation for the economy to grow by developing its natural and human resources.[5] Even his critics concede that "there is no doubt that he [Guggisberg] did a lot economically and socially for the Gold Coast".[6]

By the time the plan was introduced, the railway line from Sekondi, on the western coast, to Kumasi, in the middle of the colony, had already been completed, as well as the one from Accra to Kumasi. Guggisberg's plan was to reduce the dependence of the colony on only one major export crop, cocoa, and thus reduce the fluctuations in export revenues. This was to be done by diversifying the base of the economy through increased production of oil palm and other cash crops. By running railway lines and feeder roads through the oil palm production areas and establishing local centers for decortification and crushing of the palm nuts, it was expected that production and exports of these major crops would increase.[7] There was no intention of diminishing the role of cocoa, which had become the main export earner; rather Guggisberg's plan was to buttress the sources of revenue through diversification. In this respect, the governor was prescient. While the demand for cocoa was large and was expected to grow, it was thought that demand for the crop would be limited and subject to fluctuations. Price and export earnings fluctuations would not be useful for economic planning and development. On the other hand, the demand for both palm and kernel oil was expected to grow because of increased industrialization in Europe.

The governor saw the potential the colony had to produce several products. As Table 2.2 shows, between 1900 and 1960 the significant sources of export revenue were rubber, cocoa, and gold. The sources of export earnings varied over time. For example, between 1900 and 1905, the primary revenue source was rubber, which accounted for as much as 41% in 1900

Table 2.2 Revenue from major exports (%)

	From	*To*	*%*	*Max*	*Min*
Rubber	1900	1905	**25.46**	41.15	12.46
Cocoa	1906	1937	**59.68**	83.17	18.90
Gold	1938	1944	**49.09**	58.49	39.98
Cocoa	1945	1960	**64.33**	77.57	49.07

Source: G. B. Kay, *The Political Economy of Ghana.*

and averaged 25% of export revenues. Between 1938 and 1944, however, it was gold that earned the most export revenues for the colony. In between, and until today, it has been cocoa.

The Guggisberg plan was bold and well thought out: it was intended to lay the foundation for sustained economic growth while integrating the regions. In his speech announcing the plan, the governor described the plan as one that would assure the colony's future through increased production and exports of ground-nuts and shea butter in the north and cocoa and oil palm in the south. These four commodities – groundnuts, shea butter, oil palm, and cocoa – constituted what he called the "four large baskets". There were also what he called the "seven little baskets": rice, copra, sisal, corn, sugar, coffee, and tobacco. To accomplish the goal of diversifying the production base and increasing export revenues, the plan called for the railway line to be extended north to Tamale, from Kumasi in the center, and a deep-water port to be built at Takoradi in the southwest. These projects were meant to ensure a steady stream of revenue which would be used to tackle "education and progress" of the people (of the colony).

The scale and the far-reaching consequences of the plan can only be prop-erly appreciated by examining the expenditures proposed and the actual expen-ditures made during the period the plan was being implemented (Table 2.3).

As can be seen from Table 2.3, the total expenditure estimated for the plan period was £32,406,000. In 2018 pounds and dollars, this is £2,012,412,600 and US$2,663,629,317, respectively – a considerable sum of money both then and now.[8] By the end of the seventh year, the end point of the plan, about 62% of the amount had actually been expended; this was equal to £19,978,000, or in 2018 currencies, £1,240,633,800 or US $1,642,102,898. The major results of the expenditures were the construction of new roads, a new township (Takoradi), a new harbor (Takoradi Harbor), the extensions to the railway lines, and the construction of hospitals and schools.

The construction of the rail line into the interior boosted the exports of cocoa significantly. By 1927, cocoa accounted for 83% of export earnings – the highest it had ever been.[9] Equally important, the rail line made it easier to transport timber logs, manganese, and bauxite from the producing areas in the interior for export. These exports made the colony very rich.

The plan's emphasis on infrastructure and increasing the production of oil palm alongside cocoa was in recognition of the realities of what was happen-ing in Europe; the industrial revolution was in full bloom, and the demand for oils to constantly lubricate machinery was high. While initially most of the palm oil came from British West Africa (Nigeria and Ghana), Indonesia and Malaysia became major large producers, quickly surpassing West Africa.

Why did Ghana not continue to produce large quantities of oil palm as well as cocoa and rubber during the critical early 20th century? There is strong evidence that cocoa, rubber, and oil palm were most likely substitutes

Table 2.3 The Ten-Year Development Plan 1920–1930 expected and actual expenditures (thousands of £)

	1920–1924		1920–1930		
	1	*2*	*3*	*4*	*5 = 2 + 4*
	Estimated Expenditure	*Actual Expenditure*	*Estimated Expenditure*	*Actual Expenditure*	*Total Actual Expenditure*
Agriculture		64.00	216.00	151.00	215.00
Public Buildings	1,000.00	618.00	1,100.00	1,512.00	2,130.00
Town Improvements	420.00	211.00	1,850.00	465.00	676.00
Roads	500.00	364.00	1,000.00	1,223.00	1,587.00
Railways	3,000.00	4,139.00	14,581.00	5,821.00	9,960.00
Ports and Harbors	1,000.00	467.00	2,000.00	2,264.00	2,731.00
Post and Telegraphs	80.00	244.00	90.00	276.00	520.00
Electricity	170.00	58.00	2,000.00	188.00	246.00
Water Supplies	200.00	854.00	1,790.00	204.00	1,058.00
Takoradi/ Township			669.00	189.00	189.00
Maps and Surveys	100.00	105.00	200.00	178.00	283.00
Miscellaneous		227.00	440.00	156.00	383.00
TOTAL	**6,470.00**	**7,351.00**	**25,936.00**	**12,627.00**	**19,978.00**

Source: From table 15, p. 323 of the Statistical Abstract in G. B. Kay (1972), *The Political Economy of Colonialism in Ghana.*

as far as the farmers were concerned. All these crops are grown in the same geographical areas in the country. In 1900, oil palm, palm kernel, and rubber accounted for 83% of major export earnings. As the production of cocoa grew, the production of rubber, oil palm and palm kernel all declined and, by 1920, with cocoa accounting for over 80% of major export earnings, the combined contributions of rubber, oil palm and palm kernel had fallen to the single digits (Kay, 1972). Another reason may have been that while the cocoa was growing, farmers could interplant food crops such as plantain, banana, cassava and cocoyam (see Fora-Bah and Asafu-Adjaye, 2011). These are staple foods of the areas where cocoa was grown. It has been suggested that planting between the cocoa trees boosted their yield. On the other hand, Nuertey (1999) cites several studies to the effect that, while in the early years of oil palm growth there could be inter-cropped with food crops, as the trees developed canopies the food crops did not do very well. The cash crops did bring wealth to the farmers, but the workers needed to eat and that cost money. If they had a choice between two or three crops, and one gave them the opportunity to grow food at the same time, there is no doubt that they would choose the one they could intercrop or interplant with the food items. Over time, it may also have been the case that farmers got used to just planting cocoa and the food crops. The irony of this, which is not lost on many, is that the oil palm, which is native to West Africa and has as much potential to transform an economy as any cash crop, was replaced by cocoa, which was introduced to Ghana. Guggisberg recognized how important these crops could be for the economy, but cocoa had become too embedded to be supplanted or even complemented. Nowadays, oil palm and rubber are being grown in Ghana, but their quantities are nowhere near what they used to be or could have been.

The Guggisberg plan, in addition to its emphasis on agriculture, also spent a considerable sum of money on education and healthcare. New schools, including the famous Achimota College, which educated many of the early Ghanaian leaders, were built. Nineteen hospitals were also built, including what one could call the national hospital, Korle-Bu (now Teaching) Hospital. The existing rail lines were extended, new roads were built and old ones were reconditioned (see Kwarteng and Sosu, 2017).

The Guggisberg plan contributed significantly to the development of infrastructure in the colony. Despite seeking to increase the base of the economy by stimulating the production of other crops besides cocoa, only about 1 percent of the estimated expenditure went to agriculture. No amount went to the development of industry. One can conclude that at this time the colonial government did not see its role as being engaged in business. The government was trying to create an enabling environment for businesses (private sector). This policy was to persist for the next 44 years.

No one argues that the Ten-Year Development Plan was a failure; on the contrary, the infrastructure it created in the colony could have been one of the major reasons the Gold Coast was on the right path to sustained growth at independence.

The lessons from the Guggisberg plan are as follows:

- A well-articulated and comprehensive plan derived from a vision;
- The funds to carry out the projects in the plan;
- Capable administrator(s) to ensure that the plan stays on course or tweaked as needed;
- Stable economic and political environment.

In the Guggisberg plan, all these conditions were present. The governor was himself the visionary leader who articulated the plan. The governor came closest to the benevolent dictator described in Chapter 1, who sought to create the environment for economic development in the colony. He had the full backing of the British Colonial Office behind him.[10] The Gold Coast did not have inexhaustible funds, but it was generating a lot of revenue from the exports of the primary commodities. Between 1920 and 1927, export earnings from cocoa, gold, manganese, diamonds, timber logs, rubber, oil palm, and kernels amounted to £79,038,000 – which would be the equivalent of £4,908,259,800 or $6,496,572,671.28 in 2018. While most of the funds went to the farmers and the owners of the gold mines, who were foreigners, confidence in the Gold Coast economy enabled the government to borrow from abroad to make up for insufficient savings in the domestic economy. Indeed, the data (Kay, 1972, table 23) show that between 1920 and 1927, in only two years did government deficits occur which necessitated borrowing funds from abroad: once in 1920 and the other in 1925. Impressively, between 1920 and 1927, development accounted for 34% of the colony's expenditure. No prior period in the history of the colony had witnessed such massive government outlays on development. By 1928, it had fallen to 24%, and in the two subsequent years, it fell to 2% and 0.7%.

Finally, by 1920 the colony had been consolidated, and so there was political stability under the governance of the British. The currency in use was the British West African pound, which was pegged to the British pound at 1:1. The colony did not conduct monetary policy, and the money supply was tied directly to the foreign trade surplus. The macroeconomic conditions were sound.

The departure of Guggisberg in 1927 brought the development plan to a halt. The duration was, however, long enough for several critical aspects for it to be completed. It is important to mention that during this period a lot of surveys were done, including the survey for the development of power by damming one of the rivers. According to Birmingham, Neustadt and Omaboe (1966, p. 441), if the tempo of development between 1920 and 1927 had been maintained, Ghana would now be enjoying standards of living approaching some of the developed countries of the world.

Other plans

Between 1930 and 1963, there were no fewer than six development plans put in place; some of them overlapped and some were aborted before the endpoint: the Second Ten-Year Development Plan: 1950–1960 was ended in 1951 and folded into a Five-Year Development Plan: 1951/1952–1956/1957. A Consolidation Plan: 1957–1958 followed the Five-Year Development Plan. A Second Five-Year Development Plan: 1959–1964, which followed the Consolidation Plan was ended in 1961 and followed by the Seven-Year Development Plan: 1963/64 1969/70. It was abandoned in February 1966. We talk more about the Seven-Year Development Plan in the next section.

All plans before the Seven-Year Development Plan of 1963/1964 had emphasized developing the economy's infrastructure and improving agriculture. The need to improve agriculture before any attempt was made at manufacturing or industrialization had received a lot of attention. The Second Ten-Year Development Plan had been explicit about the government's objectives in agriculture: increase yields in the cocoa sector, increase the production of rubber and banana, lay the foundation for cattle farming, increase yields of cereals, introduce irrigation in the Volta plains, and promote the use of fertilizers. In retrospect, the emphasis on infrastructure and agricultural development was appropriate.

Increasing agricultural productivity would generate more revenue for development, and, at the same time, release labor for industry. In both the Second Ten-Year Development Plan and the Consolidated Plan, however, only about 5% of the total expenditure was allocated to improving agriculture, forestry, and fishing. The people engaged in farming and fisheries continued using traditional implements and canoes as they had for hundreds of years before.

By 1951, the government was in the hands of Gold Coasters, and the colonial government had yielded power to the Legislative Assembly, headed by the soon to be prime minister, Kwame Nkrumah. Nevertheless, one can safely assume that as long as the British were still the colonial masters, no radical departure of the economic system could have been attempted. The economy was, therefore, decidedly market-oriented and the government continued to emphasize the development of infrastructure.

Assessment

Data on how the economy fared under the various plans during the colonial period are hard to come by; a few observations can be made. Calculations using data cited by Birmingham (1967) give us an indication of how the economy was doing in the immediate pre- and post-independence era. Between 1955 and 1962, capital accumulation grew at about 8.76% and real GDP grew at about 4.87%. Between 1955 and 1960, real per capita GDP grew at about 2.65%. This was quite respectable and is about what the later, ambitious Seven-Year Development Plan (1963/1964–1970/1971) set as its growth target (2.9%).

In the nine years up to 1964, however, the *pace of growth* slowed; it fell to 3.03%. The difference between 4.87% and 3.03% is significant. At 4.87%, real GDP per capita would double in roughly every 15 years; at 3.03%, it would take about 24 years.[11] When the period is extended, the 20 years from 1955 to 1975, the per capita GDP actually barely increased, going from I$1,135.56[12] to I$1,405.21, an increase of only I$269.66. For comparison, in the same period, the Malaysian per capita GDP more than doubled, going from I$1,308.46 to I$3,030.90.

Given the sound background that had been laid in terms of infrastructure, it is difficult to explain why the economy did not fare better. A few comments might suffice. While the colonial and post-colonial economy were producing and exporting more cocoa, the world price was fluctuating and the terms of trade was deteriorating, just as had been feared by Guggisberg in the 1920s when the First Ten-Year Development Plan 1920–1930 was being deployed. In the 15-year period from the 1960/1961 crop year to the 1974/1975 crop year, there was a small but significant negative relationship between cocoa production and the world price of cocoa.[13] The price of cocoa per tonne in the 1963/1964 crop year was US$522, the same as the crop year before. In the 1964/1965 crop year, the price fell to US$389.[14] That year, Ghana produced 580,869 tons of cocoa, the most it had ever produced and would produce until 2002. Not coincidentally, the per capita GDP shrunk by 15.88% – Malaysia's per capita GDP continued to grow at 4.83%. With so much dependent on the export of one commodity, the price decrease had a significant impact on revenue and development plans.

Inability to diversify the export basket or process more of the exports was a problem that would plague the economy for some time. By 1964, the country had gone through several development plans, but the structure of the economy had not changed much. As Figure 2.1 shows, between 1955 and 1964 there was very little shift from the primary sector to the secondary

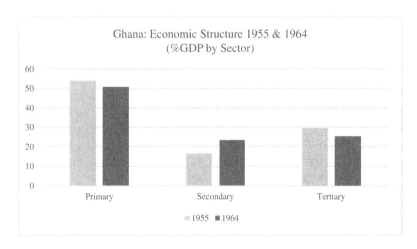

Figure 2.1 Ghana: economic structure 1959 and 1964

Source: "Economic Development of Ghana" in Birmingham, W. (1967) *Planning and Growth in Rich and Poor Countries*, Praeger, Inc., New York, NY, p. 176.

sector, and still very little from the secondary to the services or tertiary sector.

The primary sector comprises agriculture, mining, and extraction of raw materials and fishing.

The secondary sector produces finished goods (manufacturing, etc.).

The service or tertiary sector deals with the provision of intangible services.

It was not surprising that the government should seek to speed the rate of growth of the economy in the 1960s.

The Seven-Year Development Plan 1963/1964–1970/1971 and change in economic policy

The Second Five-Year Development Plan 1959–1964 to some extent marked a turning point in Ghana's economic policy. While the plan continued to emphasize the development of infrastructure, it also proposed direct government participation in industry to accelerate the rate of structural transformation from an agrarian to industrial economy. Through the pre-independence Industrial Development Corporation (IDC), several state enterprises had already been established.[15]

In a 1953 report to the Gold Coast British Colonial Government, the Nobel Laureate in Economics, Professor Arthur Lewis, had written that even though he was in favor of industrialization, he cautioned against haste. He advised that the government should first develop the agricultural sector and increase productivity, which was low: "agricultural productivity per man was stagnant". He advised that tackling low productivity should be the number one priority and gave three reasons:

1   The increased productivity could release labor for industry;
2   If industrialization was not to depend on foreign capital, which Lewis argued could be attracted only at unfavorable terms, then it would have to come from the increased savings that could be made possible from increased agricultural productivity and the taxes that could be levied;
3   Finally, the domestic market for manufactured/industrial products was too small at that time.

For these reasons, while Lewis did not discourage industrialization, he concluded that it should not be the number one priority. Among the list of seven things Lewis had suggested the government should do in order to carry out an industrialization program, one of them was for the government "to operate government owned factories" (Lewis, Chapter 5 #241(g)). One can debate whether this was the impetus for the massive establishment of the

many state enterprises that were subsequently set up or whether the rec-
ommendation happened to coincide with what the Ghana government had
already concluded about how the economy should be developed. At any rate,
beginning with the Second Five-Year Development Plan (1959–1964), and
reinforced by the Seven-Year Development Plan (1963/1964–1970/1971),
the orientation of the economy began to change. The presence of the state in
activities that had hitherto been limited or dominated by the private sector
began to proliferate. The Second Five-Year Development Plan sought to
fundamentally alter the laissez-faire economy inherited from colonial times
and before; the mantra of the plan was industrialization in the context of a
socialist economy.

In the March 1964 speech that launched the Seven-Year Plan for National
Reconstruction and Development 1963/1964–1969/1970, popularly known
as the Seven-Year Development Plan (SYDP), the stated goals of the Plan
were threefold, to:

1   Speed the rate of growth of the economy;
2   Embark upon the *socialist transformation of the economy* through the
    rapid development of the State and cooperative sectors;
3   Eradicate completely the *colonial structure* of the economy.

Further, it was felt that the country would be hampering its "advance to
socialism if [it] were to encourage the growth of Ghanaian private capitalism". The government indicated that it would encourage "the small busi-
nessman who employs his capital in an industry or trade with which he
is familiar, and in so doing fulfills a public need". What was not going to
be encouraged however, was the type of business where individuals "use
their money, not in productive endeavor", but to buy and resell "at high
prices, such commodities as fish, salt and other items of food and consumer
goods which are in demand by the people". This type of business was seen
as "colonial exploitation". In its place, state enterprises and cooperatives
would be established. To that end, the plan called for the expansion and the
addition of several state-owned enterprises.

A clear industrial policy was also discernible from the SYDP, that of
import substitution industrialization (ISI). The policy can be gleaned from
the type of industries that were established or which the plan intended to
set up; mostly food, textiles, footwear, fertilizers, and building materials.
The raw materials for these light industries were capable of being produced
locally. The problem with ISI, as has been noted by many economists, is
that it often comes with controls: tariffs and quotas, import licensing, out-
right bans of imports, and foreign exchange controls. These are all meant to
protect the newly established *infant industries*. The absence of competition

from foreign products often means that the infants never grow up, and when they are forced to compete with foreign products, they are found to be wanting and do not survive. If that happens, then the resources that went into setting them up have been wasted. The foundation for these policies in Ghana, although laid in the 1960s, continued well into the 1980s, and some would argue that it still haunts the economy. The SYDP did recognize some other problems: As the industries expand, which they will as the economy grows, the demand for raw materials will increase; unless these raw materials are produced locally, these increases in demand will lead to increases in imports of raw materials and cause net exports to decrease. Therefore, a wise course of action would be to start with the industries that process the raw materials that constitute the bulk of the country's exports; these industries would have a relatively low import content (SYDP p. 222) and therefore avert the problem. Again, this would suggest that agricultural productivity should be increased.

Over the plan period, it was projected that the real GDP would grow at 5.5% a year. With the population expected to grow at about 2.6% a year (SYDP p. 240) over the period, real GDP per capita will then grow at about 2.9% (5.5% minus 2.6%). To achieve these numbers, the country needed domestic savings of 15% of GDP and a further 5% from abroad to make up 20%. The government also planned to use deficit financing (essentially printing money) to supplement the sources of funds for development.

In the five years preceding the launching of the plan in 1964, the average gross domestic savings had been 13.56% of GDP[16] – shy of the 15% required; foreign capital inflow had also fallen short of the 5% mark. Nonetheless, the planners felt confident that the growth of new sources of foreign capital, such as the African Development Bank, could help finance some of the self-liquidating parts of the plan. Moreover, while domestic savings in the preceding three years had been lower than what the plan called for, it had been 17.15% in 1960 and 15.53% in 1964. The target was, therefore, not unrealistic. The major problem was that the demand for the most important primary product which Ghana exported, cocoa, and which produced the bulk of government tax revenue, was demand inelastic. As observed elsewhere, an increase in production tended to decrease the price, and hence the revenue. The need for diversifying the basket of exported goods was critical, and it did not appear that care had been taken in ensuring that the basket was diversified enough, as the Guggisberg Plan and the Lewis Report had suggested.

The government continued to develop infrastructure. Between 1959 and 1964, during the Second Five-Year Development Plan, about 22% of the £G179.587 million (Ghana pounds) were spent on the construction of a second seaport at Tema (Tema Harbor) and about 2.3% for the development of a new township (Tema). Foreign and domestic funds were also assembled to bring the Volta River Hydro-Electric Project (Volta Dam) to life. These two projects, the Volta Dam and the second port at Tema, constituted the most significant infrastructure during the period. The government saw the Volta River Hydro-electric Project, administered by the Volta River Authority (VRA), as an essential part of the long-range plan to develop the country.

The Volta Dam, however, would not have been economically feasible without the anticipated huge demand for electric power from the aluminum smelter plant, Volta Aluminum Company (VALCO), that was constructed at Tema to process alumina into aluminum. The plan also envisaged the construction of an alumina plant to convert bauxite into alumina, instead of exporting the raw bauxite and importing the alumina back to be processed into aluminum. This would have produced the kind of vertical integration and job creation that would have increased the value added to bauxite. The alumina plant (to process bauxite into alumina) was never built; the foreign partners did not see the need to construct one in Ghana when they had other plants elsewhere which could supply the alumina to Ghana. VALCO (to process alumina into aluminum smelter) made the Volta Dam a good enough economic proposition to garner financial support from the World Bank.[17]

The general outline of SYDP clearly showed a comprehensive plan for development, but the scale of the projects to be undertaken and the large and speedy intrusion of the government into what used to be a market economy meant that the government would not have enough funds to spend on critical infrastructure. And at the same time, it would not have enough time to develop the expertise to manage the projects and/or would manage them inefficiently. Further, the government had already recognized the fact that the country did not have enough technical or managerial expertise and that it needed to train more people. Yet, the plan proceeded as if all these were in place.

That the SYDP was ambitious is borne out by the fact that the total planned expenditure over the seven-year period was 250% greater than the combined expenditure of the two plans from 1951 to 1959 (which was £G135.8 million). Planned expenditure under the SYDP was £G475.5 million.[18] As Table 2.4 shows, about 32% was allocated for the provision of social services, of which education was the major component. The next major expenditure component was public infrastructure, to which about 26% of the total expenditure was allocated. The plan also envisioned the completion of the Volta Dam.

Industry and mining accounted for 23% and agriculture 14%. What made the plan a stand was the large number of state-owned- enterprises (SOEs): What had already been completed (3), what had begun (10), and the ones for which commitments had been made or were under consideration (about 53). The complexes, factories, mills, and plants ranged from food to pharmaceuticals, chemicals to metallurgical, raw material preparations to building

Table 2.4 Seven-Year Development Plan: planned expenditure % distribution

Sector	% of Estimated Expenditure	£G Millions
Social Services	31.61	150.3
Infrastructure	25.85	122.9
Industry and Mining	22.99	109.3
Agriculture	14.30	68.0
Miscellaneous	5.26	25.0
Total	**100.00**	**475.50**

Source: SYDP, p. 27.

materials and assembly of finished products. The SYDP is a good example of the Big Push model for industrialization in practice. As noted by Rosenstein-Rodan (1943), "complementarity of different industries provides the best set of arguments in favor of large-scale planned industrialization", such as the SYDP was trying to do in Ghana.

In agriculture, for example, small-scale farmers had always produced most of the crops for domestic consumption and export. Cocoa, which was, and is still, the major export crop, is produced by farmers on lot sizes varying between 5 and 7 hectares (4 to 12 acres).[19] The SYDP called for the establishment of state and co-operative farms, and because they were large, they were to be mechanized. According to Miracle and Seidman (1968), the problems that the state farms faced in the 1960s were the same as those faced by the first attempt at mechanized farming in the northern part of Ghana in the 1950s. The terrain was not suitable for the equipment; spare parts had to be imported, which required scarce foreign exchange; the minimum efficient scale of operation was still large, and many of the farms could not achieve that minimum. The result was that productivity was in many cases lower than the small-scale individually owned farms. According to Due (1969), 1,205 state and institutional farms were established to increase production, but in spite of the large investment and large tracts of land acquired and cleared, only 1.2% was cultivated in 1964, and by 1965 only 1.4% had been cultivated.[20] Many of the state farms were discontinued shortly after 1966. They never made the expected impact.

The need to increase productivity in agriculture has always being priority number one. Increased output and productivity would provide the raw materials for the new agribusinesses that had already been established (e.g., oil and rice mills) or were planned; release labor to go into other sectors of the economy; and generate additional savings for other sectors of the economy. A cautious approach would have been to increase farm productivity first and ensure that production would be dependable before the factories were established. The use of improved seeds and fertilizers could probably have accomplished a lot more than the wholesale adoption of large state farms. The change to large-scale mechanized farming was a radical departure from the traditional ways in which crops had been produced in the country. Not since the 1950s had the government tried to establish state farms. Unfortunately, in both cases, the results were unsuccessful.

The very short period of 1963/1964 to 1966 of the plan's implementation was probably a lost window of opportunity for takeoff in Ghana. There was a lot of goodwill for the newly independent nation of Ghana. The infrastructure was relatively better than surrounding countries' revenues from cocoa, gold and the other minerals, still provided the means to industrialize, albeit slowly. The speed and scale with which the SYDP sought to transform the economy did not yield the results desired in terms of economic growth. Inability to diversify the export base meant export revenues, the source for the acquisition of machinery for industrialization, could not be relied upon.

The five-year growth rates (shown in Table 2.5) show that per capita GDP did not grow much during the period of the SYDP or thereafter. It must be recalled that the SYDP sought to increase real GDP per capita by 2.9% annually. Between 1961 and 1965, a time frame roughly encompassing the plan period, the growth rate declined. Between 1963 and 1966, when the plan began and ended, it fell by 2.03%.

While there are some serious doubts about whether the plan had any chance of succeeding, other factors contributed to making sure that it would not. In the first full year of the plan, between 1963/1964 and 1964/1965, the world

Table 2.5 Five-year growth rates of real GDP/capita: constant 2010 US$

Five-Year Period	Growth Rate (%)
1961–1965	−0.05
1966–1970	0.43
1971–1975	−2.33
1976–1980	−1.48
1981–1985	−2.67
1986–1990	1.81
1991–1995	1.65
1996–2000	0.64
2001–2005	2.93
2006–2010	4.60
2011–2015	5.80
2016–2017	4.59

Source: https://data.worldbank.org/indicator/NY.GDP.MKTP.KD?locations=MY.

Table 2.6 Cocoa price fluctuations: Ghana

Crop Year	Price/Tonne (US$)	% Δ Price	Output	% Δ Output	Receipts	% Δ Receipts
1963/1964	522		427,782		223,302,204	
1964/1965	389	−25.48	580,869	35.79	225,958,041	1.19
1965/1966	491	26.22	415,762	−28.42	204,139,142	−9.66

Sources: https://cocobod.gh/weakly_purchase.php, International Cocoa Organization, QBCS, Vol. XLII No. 1, Cocoa year 2015/16.

price of cocoa dropped by more than 25% per tonne. Receipts from sales went up only because production increased by about 36%. In the event, total receipts increased by only one percent. In the 1965/1966 crop year, however, even though prices recovered by 26%, it was still below the 1963/1964 high of US$522, and with a decrease in production of 28% that year, receipts fell by about 10% (see Table 2.6). These fluctuations in foreign exchange receipts of the major export crop make plan implementation difficult.

In 1960, cocoa accounted for about 59% of Ghana's exports, followed by timber and logs (14%), gold (10%), diamonds (9%) and manganese (6%). By 1967, the dependence on cocoa had increased to 65%. The failure to diversify the basket of exports meant that variations in the one crop, cocoa, were transmitted to the entire economy with disastrous effects.

One could also argue that the plan was doomed to fail because it was too ambitious and the necessary groundwork was not in place; there was an absence of sufficient managerial and technical expertise, inadequate and unsteady supply of inputs, and so forth. During the period the plan was being implemented, real GDP per capita actually fell. It may very well have been that not enough time had passed to give the plan a chance to succeed. Those who argue that the plan was successful cite the fact that it provided needed critical infrastructure upon which later development would depend. The lasting impact of the period was the tilt in the orientation of the economy towards state-directed and controlled industrialization; this was to persist for a long time. The country continued in this direction well into the mid-1980s. By this time, the gap between economic development in Ghana and Malaysia had widened considerably.

The post–Seven-Year Development Plan and economic policies in Ghana

The period between 1966 and 2001 was characterized by instability, and fear of instability, in Ghana. The country alternated between military and civilian governments until 2001, each regime being short-lived. Four development plans were introduced during the period, but none had the same transformative impact that previous plans had. The per capita real GDP grew by an anemic 0.69% a year. The real GDP/capita had inched up to I$1,477.92. By all accounts, the economy had not begun the takeoff. Four development plans were introduced; none of the plans had the same impact on the economy as the SYDP and the Guggisberg Plan. The Two-Year 'Stabilization Plan" (1967/1968 to 1968/1969) sought to shift development from the urban areas to the rural areas with emphasis on agriculture. The Rural Development Plan (1971–1972) tried to increase the per capita income to at least $3,000 by 2020. The Ghana Shared Growth and Development Agenda (GSGDA) (2010–2013), as the name implied, was to increase the rate of growth of the economy to at least 8%, and ensure that the benefits of economic growth would be fairly shared (GSGDA pp. 1–2).

One can divide Ghana's effort at economic development into many phases or periods. Here is one such categorization:

1   The period before independence, when the economy was decidedly market driven, and the colonial government provided the infrastructure necessary to meet the needs of the only private extractive businesses. Government expenditure matched its receipts and development was financed mainly by government revenues.

2   The period between 1951 and 1957, when the British transferred internal administration to the colony and economic policy followed what pertained in period 1.

3   The period between 1957 and 1965, when the government embarked on the transformation of the economy by changing the tilt from a market-driven laissez-faire one to a socialist economy: the state owning resources, producing and distributing goods and services.

4   The period between 1966 and 2001, characterized by instability and uncertainties in governance, and no clear sense of direction as to whether to continue the socialist agenda or to revert to a market economy. This period also saw a continuation of restrictive economic policies, foreign exchange controls, scarcities, and general economic malaise, at least until the mid-1980s when the liberalization began.

5   The period after 2001, characterized by stability and a return to market-oriented economic policies.

With the return to a democratic and a free-market economy, a new problem emerged. A vibrant democracy also meant that governments could change every four or eight years, and so could economic policy. In anticipation of this, Section V Articles 86 and 87 of the 1992 Ghana Constitution established a National Development Planning Commission (NDPC) to ensure that there would be continuity in development plan implementation. Plans are only as good as the planners behind them and the personnel to monitor and implement them thoroughly. Without expertise in human resources, good plans count for naught. Development plans continue to be launched in Ghana to this day, but they often lack continuity. The latest is a 40-year development plan, in 2015/2016.[21]

Colonial and immediate post-colonial economic policies: Malaysia

Introduction

When we talk of Malaysia, we are essentially limiting ourselves to the entity that emerged after 1965 when Singapore left the Federation. This entity still includes the Eastern States of Sarawak and Sabah. Malaysia does have some slight natural advantages over Ghana. Virtually the whole country, both Peninsular and East Malaysia, is surrounded by water, which lowers transportation costs. At its widest point, Peninsular Malaysia is about 200 miles wide; this means that no point on the peninsula is more than 100 miles from water. The biggest state, Sarawak, is located on Eastern Malaysia, which shares a border with Indonesia to the south, and the farthest point from the South China Sea to the north is 204 miles.

Like Ghana, Malaysia is naturally well endowed. It is currently the 28th largest oil-producing country in the world, with proven reserves of four billion barrels as of January 2011. Also, it is ranked as the country with the 14th largest gas reserves, with 88 trillion standard cubic feet. While the endowment of natural resources can sometimes lead to what is known as the "resource curse",[22] Malaysia has been able to leverage the natural resource endowment into robust, diversified economic growth. Indeed, according to the Economic Planning Unit (EPU), the country is now actively positioning itself as a technology hub and discouraging labor-intensive methods of production in favor of capital and knowledge-intensive methods. This is partly to curb the influx of unskilled workers who tend to dilute wages, and partly because this is where the most value can be added.

Malaysia's economic performance since independence has put it in a class all by itself, with some economic historians regarding it as one of the most successful countries that has achieved a "relatively smooth transition to modern growth in the last century or so".[23] The World Bank ranks it among the upper-middle-income countries; Ghana is a lower-middle-income country. The rankings, however, do not tell the whole story; the real per capita GDP of Malaysia is about six times higher than that of Ghana as of 2017. That was not always the case. From 1955 to 1964, the real GDP per capita of Ghana was larger than that of Malaysia. It was not until 1965 that Malaysia's real GDP per capita became higher than Ghana's.

Between 1965 and 1984, a period of 20 years, Malaysia's real GDP per capita grew at an average of 7.95%. At that rate, the real GDP per capita was doubling about every ten years. In 1964, the real GDP per capita was US$3,034.28. By 1984, it had increased to US$8,409.12.

As indicated earlier, the Ghanaians encouraged the colonial officers to leave almost immediately after independence. The departure of such senior officers could not have been good for the economy. On the other hand, according to Navaratnam (1997), Malaysia proceeded slowly, continuing the laissez-faire policies of the colonial era. Rather than indigenizing the economy immediately after independence as Ghana did, Malaysia allowed senior British officers to stay, and they "served for many years providing good training and guidance and continuity". The Malaysian economy remained open with a liberal foreign exchange regime. The slow approach to development in the early stages and the preservation of the market orientation of the economy engendered confidence and served to encourage foreign investment. Table 2.7 shows that between 1970 and 2009, foreign direct investment (FDI) as a percent of GDP in Malaysia exceeded that of Ghana in every period except 2000 to 2009. More importantly, as shown in Table 2.8, in absolute terms, the flow of FDI to Malaysia exceeded that of Ghana many times, reaching a high of 73.28:1 between 1980 and 1989.

Table 2.7 Foreign direct investment (% of GDP)

Period	Malaysia	Ghana	Ratio: Malaysia/Ghana
1970–1979	3.78	.53	7.1
1980–1989	3.10	.18	17.1
1990–1999	5.83	1.72	3.4
2000–2009	2.97	3.80	0.78

Source: World Development Indicators, World Bank.

Note: 1970 to 1979 average for Ghana includes data for only 1975–1979.

Table 2.8 Foreign direct investment (FDI): 2011 national prices (millions of US$)

Period	Malaysia (MYS)	Ghana (GHA)	MYS/GHA
1970–1979	249,158.97	15,233.99	16.36
1980–1989	390,086.90	5,323.17	73.28
1990–1999	1,497,992.74	75,882.99	19.74
2000–2009	1,269,574.83	266,211.81	4.77

Source: World Development Indicators, World Bank.

One could argue that the preservation of the colonial economic structure meant that the interests of private businesses, primarily British and Chinese, who had dominated the economy before independence, remained intact; and that this may have stoked tensions among the majority Malays and the poor, contributing to the later ethnic conflicts.

The go-slow approach also meant that the Malaysian government did not have to borrow excessively and use deficit financing to the same degree to undertake large-scale projects as Ghana did. Instead, Malaysia relied on domestic savings and FDI. The result was a sound macroeconomic environment characterized by price stability, a stable foreign exchange rate, and a liberal open economy that engendered confidence and thus contributed to FDI.

The initial emphasis on exports seemed to have worked to help the economy grow. From 1967 to 1980, the trade balance in Malaysia remained in surplus, boosted in part by the export of its major primary commodities. Exports grew an average of 6.57% a year. Even though imports also grew at 6.07% a year, the average trade balance a year was RM 2,102.4 million. This surplus would ensure that there would be no undue pressure on the exchange rate and more importantly, that there would be macroeconomic stability; price stability, low and stable interest rates, a stable foreign exchange rate, and the accumulation of reserves to ensure that the central bank could step in when needed to stabilize the economy.

While the policy of continuing the laissez-faire of the colonial era meant that the interests of private foreign businesses (mostly British) were protected, it buttressed the economic power of the Chinese minority who were also in the private sector (Varatnam, 1997). According to Sundaram and Hui (2014, p. 12), the policy during the early period after independence precluded the government from interfering in commerce and industry. The government did, however, attempt to bring the indigenous Malays (about 60% of the population), into the mainstream of economic activity. It did so by investing in rural development and education. This benefited the indigenous Malays since they tended to live in rural areas and were mostly engaged in fishing and farming.

Promoting rural development in agriculture presented some difficulties. The large plantations were in the hands of influential private landlords, and the government could not be seen as actively engaged in that sector. How the government went about solving the problem provides a lesson in transformation that many developing countries have tried unsuccessfully to emulate.

Planning and economic policy

Economic planning in Malaysia dates back to the 1950s, before independence. For the most part, it was not as intrusive as Ghana's became in the late 1950s and early 1960s. The plans laid out broad national goals and gave the private sector room to operate within them. Lee and Chew-Ging (2017) provide an excellent narration of the various development plans implemented in Malaysia since 1950. The plans were typically five-year plans and were not static; details were changed to meet changing economic circumstances. In 1961, the Economic Planning Unit (EPU) was established and charged with development planning, and execution.[24]

The first four development plans of Malaysia (the Draft Plan 1950–1955, the First Malaya Plan 1956–1960, the Second Malaya Plan 1961–1965, and the Third Malaysia Plan 1966–1970) emphasized the provision of social services, infrastructure, rural development, diversification of the economy, employment creation, racial harmonization, population planning, and economic growth. Since the government did not want to be directly involved in commerce, industry, or agriculture, the Federal Land Development Authority (FELDA) was set up under the Land Development Ordinance Act. As explained to the authors on their field visit to one of the settlements in Pahang in the summer of 2018, the idea was to provide an opportunity for the marginally employed and unemployed to empower themselves by allocating land for them to cultivate oil palm and rubber plantations. Each settler was allotted 10 hectares (24.7 acres) of land to cultivate. The government, through FELDA, provided the land and basic infrastructure (schools, extension services, etc.), and settlers built their houses and planted the crops. As of 1990, FELDA was to be financially self-sufficient. In 2011, it expanded into other businesses, while some of the successful settlers also branched into other economic activities on or off the settlements.[25] Although most of the settlers were indigenous Malays, there were some Chinese and Indians among them. Indications are that the program was a success. While the initiative was from the government – it provided the land and the infrastructure and the necessary extension services – the private initiative of the settlers determined the success or failure of the project as well as the settlers' own prosperity.

Another institution that had an impact on the transformation of the Malaysian economy was the Malaysian Investment Development Authority (MIDA). Established during the period of implementation of the First Malaysia Plan 1966–1970, restructuring of the Malaysian economy was the purpose of the Malaysian Investment Development Authority (MIDA), previously called the Malaysian Industrial Development Authority (also MIDA). MIDA was established in 1965 and became operational in 1967 as a 'One Stop Center" for taking care of FDI. It is the first point of contact for investors in the country: "MIDA assists companies which intend to invest in the manufacturing and services sectors, as well as facilitates the implementation of their projects".[26]

MIDA is intended to make foreign investments in Malaysia as easy as possible. One of the ways it does this is to station senior representatives from key government agencies at the headquarters in Kuala Lumpur "to advise investors on government policies and procedures". The entities at the head-quarters include personnel from the Immigration Office, Customs Office, Labor Department, utility companies (telephone and power), environment, and customs. In addition to explaining to prospective investors where to get what, MIDA also advises investors on opportunities in the country.

From 1955 to 1965, a period that encompassed the first three of these plans, real GDP grew an average of 5.54% and per capita real GDP at 2.39%. The slower growth in real GDP per capita was the result of the population increasing at over 3.0% a year and therefore diluting the gains. From 1955 to 2007, Malaysia exported more goods than it imported (balance of trade in goods was in surplus for the period), except for the years 1981 and 1982.[27] During the same period, the current account fluctuated but was in aggregate a surplus between 1955 and 2007. That fact indicates that the government policy of diversifying the economy and focusing on exports as a means to promote growth was achieving success. Rather than focus on import sub-stitution by itself, it was coupled with exports: import-substitution-export-oriented growth.

The next four plans, spanning 20 years, transformed the *economy* into a diversified self-sustaining one. The Second Malaysia Plan 1966–1970, Third Malaysia Plan 1971–1975, Fourth Malaysia Plan 1975–1980, and Fifth Malaysia Plan 1986–1990 are collectively referred to as the New Eco-nomic Policy (NEP). The beginning of the plan coincided with the worst racial riots Malaysia had ever experienced, the 1969 Ethnic Conflicts. The First Malaysia Plan had set as its goals racial harmonization, economic growth, employment generation, economic diversification, and population planning. The Malays, largely confined to the rural areas and shut out of the mainstream of economic activities, had consoled themselves with holding political power. Ethnic capital holdings show that foreigners held a greater proportion of capital in Malaysia than any indigenous group. Data compiled by Sundaram and Hui (2014 p. 89) and abridged in Table 2.9 show that non-Bumiputeras still hold a higher proportion of capital and thus economic power than Bumiputeras. For example, in 1970, 63.4% of the ownership of shares in limited companies was held by foreigners and 28.3% by non-Bumiputeras, while the majority Bumiputeras (over 50% of the population) held 2.4%. There has been some progress since the 1970s. As of 2008, the Bumiputeras' share had risen to about 22%. At the same time, the share owned by the Chinese increased to 34.9% from 27.2% (1970). The share of foreign holdings has fallen from 63.4% to 37.9%

Ensuring that income inequality is minimized is the goal of all gov-ernments. Where the source of income is an asset, such as land, which is monopolized by one group, redressing initial inequity can sometime wreak

Table 2.9 Percent share ownership in limited companies by ethnicity

Ethnicity	1970	1990	2000
Bumiputera	*2.40%*	*19.30%*	*18.90%*
Individuals	1.60	14.20	14.2
Institutions	0.80	5.10	3.00
Trust Agencies			1.70
Non-Bumiputera	*28.20*	*46.80*	*41.30*
Chinese	27.20	45.50	38.90
Indians	1.00	1.00	1.50
Others		0.30	0.90
Nominee Companies	*6.00*	*8.50*	*8.50*
Foreigners	*63.40*	*25.40*	*31.30*
Total	100.00	100.00	100.00

Source: Sundaram and Hui (2014, p. 89).

havoc on an economy. Recent examples include land distribution in Zimbabwe and South Africa. Attempts to redistribute land in Zimbabwe after independence from white settlers to Africans has been the root cause of the difficulties facing Zimbabwe. In the case of Malaysia, it was the recognition that without giving the majority Bumiputeras access to capital and therefore seats in the boardrooms, there could be no societal harmony and economic progress.

Racial harmonization, as part of government policy, could not have come sooner. In May 1969, Malaysia experienced its worst ethnic conflicts, primarily between the majority Malays and the second-largest ethnic group, the Chinese.[28] In the wake of the crisis, the government began in earnest to adopt development plans that were inclusive of all sectors of the economy, especially the poor in the rural areas who also happen to be predominantly Malays. The 20-year plan covering the period 1971 to 1990, broken into the five-year plans described earlier, had multiple goals: the eradication of poverty; restructuring of the economy; revitalization of the agricultural sector; movement into heavy industry; and the privatization of state institutions. All this had to happen in the context of a private economy.

We mentioned earlier that in the period immediately before and after independence up until 1964, the real GDP per capita of Ghana was greater than that of Malaysia. In 1964, the real per capita GDP of Ghana was US$3,067.45 and US$3,034.28 in Malaysia. The rate at which the Malaysian economy grew between 1958 and 1970 (5.98%) was already greater than the rate at which the Ghanaian economy was growing, which was 4.23%. After 1970, however, the gap in the growth rates became even bigger. Between 1971 and

1984, Malaysia experienced another growth spurt, the real GDP surging at 8.85% compared to Ghana's decline of 0.13%.

The growth in Malaysia was the result of the rapid increase in exports, the increase in domestic savings, and the increase in FDI. The 50-year period between 1967 and 2016 saw exports grow at a rate of 12.4% annually.[29] During the same period, the trade balance was positive in all but seven years. The surpluses led to an accumulation of reserves close to US$2 billion between 1970 and 1975.

What did Malaysia do differently?

One cannot understate the impact stability has had on Malaysia's economic growth compared to Ghana. While it is true that the country has suffered many conflicts, it has through it all maintained enough stability for the economy to grow. Since independence in 1957, the ruling coalition has always been dominated by the United Malays National Organization (UMNO) formed in 1946. While there have always been opposition parties, the successor to the Alliance, Barisan Nasional, has always remained in power, providing the necessary stability and continuity to start and finish development projects. Development plans need economic and political stability; a stable fiscal environment reduces risks and therefore increases foreign investment.

As early as 1961, the federation of the Malaysian government established the (Malaysian) National Planning Development Committee (MNPDC) with the Economic Planning Unit (EPU) as its secretariat. Although the cabinet (politicians) retained ultimate control of the planning process, the MNPDC with the EPU as its secretariat had "the responsibility for the formulation, implementation, progress evaluation and revision of development plans".[30] Ghana had done something similar in the past; under Articles 86 and 87 of the 1992 Constitution, the (Ghana) National Development Planning Commission (GNDPC) was set up as an advisory body to the president. The GNDPC's tasks are to help the government develop, coordinate, and monitor development policies, but only as an advisory body. The Malaysian EPU was not set up as an advisory unit, but rather as the entity that initiates, executes, monitors and revises plans. These tasks were made easier by two important factors: (1) the EPU reported directly to the prime minister and therefore had considerable influence in getting the full cooperation of all ministries, including the most important, the Treasury, which funds the plans; and (2) the same party or alliance had been in power for a long period, maintaining continuity in vision, planning, execution and monitoring.

As we discuss in the next chapter, households, businesses, and economies become wealthy by saving. The more an economy saves, the more capital it can acquire to equip workers to enable them to produce more in total and per person. The savings can come from two sources: households and governments in the domestic economy, which constitutes the national savings, and foreigners.

To increases savings, the Malaysian government set up institutions that provided incentives for the poor to save. Of these, the most notable was the Permodalan Nasional Berhad (PNB), which was set up in 1978.[31] The goals of PNB were as follows: make it possible for Malays, who had traditionally, been shut off from corporate Malaysia, to increase their participation in it by buying units in PNB; and equally important, mobilize domestic savings at the same time.

The precise mechanics of how PNB managed to convince Malays, many of whom lived in the rural areas, to open 13 million[32] accounts is beyond the scope of this text. Suffice it to say, PNB succeeded in mobilizing domestic savings with which it was able to buy units in corporations, and thus provide representations for the Bumiputeras on corporate boards.

Conclusion

If one were to draw preliminary conclusions about what policies Malaysia pursued to make its economy grow so much faster than the Ghanaian economy in the roughly 60 years plus after independence in 1957, one would include factors such as the slow and steady approach adopted by its government, and the continuation of colonial policies after independence and the stability of the post-independence ruling coalition government. These policies *provided continuity in the pursuit of economic policies and at the same time induced confidence for foreign investors*. The creation of institutions to mobilize domestic savings, and policies that increased exports of goods and were also significant factors. Comparatively, Ghana's hasty plan to indigenize its economy and grow faster in a short period of time may have hurt its ability to handle its economy properly. Its inability to diversify its exports and dependence on one major export crop, cocoa, the vacillation between a centrally planned and market economy, and instability in government over the period all combined to create a risky environment for foreign investment and for business.

In Chapters 4 and 5, we survey the literature to identify the factors that caused the disparity in growth performances in the two economies.

Notes

1 The wars or skirmishes were over control of trade routes and land concessions.
2 Lower-middle-income economies are those with a GNI per capita between $996 and $3,895; upper-middle-income economies are those with a GNI per capita between $3,896 and $12,055.

www.worldbank.org/en/news/feature/2011/07/18/ghana-looks-to-retool-its-economy-as-it-reaches-middle-income-status, accessed 6/17/2019.

3 www.britannica.com/place/western-Africa/The-beginnings-of-European-activity, accessed 2/9/2019.

4 Report of the Mission to the Gold Coast, February 4, 1957, International Bank for Reconstruction and Development, Department of Operations, Europe, African and Australasia.

5 The implementation actually ended in 1927, the year the governor left Ghana.

6 Agbodeka, Francis, "Sir Gordon Guggisberg's Contribution to the Development of the Gold Coast, 1919–1927", *Transactions of the Historical Society of Ghana*, Vol. 13, No. 1 (June 1972), pp. 51–64, published by Historical Society of Ghana, www.jstor.org/stable/pdf/41405804.pdf, accessed 5/15/2019.

7 Governor's Annual Address, *Legislative Council Debates*, 1921–1922, pp. 29–48, from G. B. Kay's *The Political Economy of Colonialism in Ghana: A Collection of Statistics*, Cambridge, UK, Cambridge University Press, 1972.

8 We use the relative price from Officer and Williamson's "Five Ways to Compute Relative Value of a U.K. Pound Amount from 1270 to Present", www.measuringworth.com/ukcompare/. £1.00 in 1930 is worth £62.1 in 2018. We also convert the sterling into US dollars using www.poundsterlinglive.com/best-exchange-rates, all accessed on 5/15/2019. In 2018, the rate between the dollar and sterling was £1 = US$1.323236, the mid-exchange rate.

9 The total earnings from cocoa alone in 1927 were £11,272,000, which in 2019 US dollars is equivalent to $28,506,888,000. One (£1) 1927 is equal to 2019 US$2,529 – no paltry sum of money even today. www.likeforex.com/currency-converter/british-sterling-pound-gbp_usd-us-dollar.htm/1927, accessed 5/1/2019.

10 www.britishempire.co.uk/biography/guggisberg.htm, accessed 5/15/2019. This brief biography reveals the extent to which he felt he could do good for the colonies and how committed he was to his cause.

11 Rule of 72 (72/4.87).

12 An international dollar would buy in the cited country a comparable amount of goods and services a US dollar would buy in the United States. This term is often used in conjunction with Purchasing Power Parity (PPP) data. World Bank definition.

13 Calculated using data from https://cocobod.gh/weakly_purchase.php, accessed 2/18/2016 and *Quarterly Bulletin of Cocoa Statistics*, Vol. XLII, No. 1, Cocoa Year 2015/2016.

14 A (metric) tonne is about 1.10 tons.

15 The Industrial Development Corporation's mandate included the establishment of "new industrial undertakings, supply the entire capital and taking full control of the management" (see Kay (1972) p. 92).

16 World Bank national accounts data, and OECD National Accounts data files.

17 "Appraisal of The Volta River Hydroelectric Project, Ghana", August 30, 1961, IBRD, Department of Technical Operations.

18 This is equivalent to £9,546.16 million (US$11,968.59 million) in 2019, assuming 1 Ghanaian pound in 1964 was equal to 1 pound sterling. www.in2013dollars.com/uk/inflation/1964?amount=475, accessed 6/19/2019.

19 https://cocoainitiative.org/news-media-post/cocoa-farmers-in-ghana-experience-poverty-and-economic-vulnerability/, accessed 6/19/2019.

20 State Farms Corporation had 123, Workers Brigade had 47, Young Farmers League had 37, and other institutions had 128.

21 www.graphic.com.gh/features/opinion/a-40-year-national-vision-or-development-plan-for-ghana.html, accessed 6/28/2019.
22 Sometimes also called the paradox of plenty: the tendency for countries with an abundance of non-renewable natural resources to perform worse in economic development than those with less.
23 Drabble, John, "The Economic History of Malaysia". EH.Net Encyclopedia, edited by Robert Whaples, July 31, 2004, http://eh.net/encyclopedia/economic-history-of-malaysia/, accessed 9/6/2019.
24 https://knoema.com/atlas/sources/EPU, accessed 7/24/2019.
25 www.felda.gov.my/en/public/felda/milestones, accessed 7/22/2019.
26 www.mida.gov.my/home/about-mida/posts/, accessed 8/3/2019.
27 www.dosm.gov.my/v1/uploads/files/3_Time%20Series/Malaysia_Time_Series_2015/02BOP.pdf, table 2.1, accessed 7/27/2019.
28 For more on the conflict, described as the worst, Soong Kua Kia, "Racial Conflict in Malaysia: Against the Official History", *Institute of Race Relations*, Sage Publications, Vol. 49, no. 3 (2007), pp. 33–53.
29 www.dosm.gov.my/v1/uploads/files/3_Time%20Series/Malaysia_Time_Series_2015/02BOP.pdf, accessed 7/21/2019.
30 https://knoema.com/atlas/sources/EPU, accessed 8/3/2019.
31 Permodalan in English means capitalization, but it is probably better translated as capital mobilization. In our conversations with the head of corporate affairs, it was explained to us that it is a national equity bank.
32 www.pnb.com.my/about_e.php, accessed 8/3/2019. In July 2018 when we visited PNB headquarters in Kuala Lumpur, we were told that PNB currently manages a fund of RM280 billion or US$64.2 billion (at RM1 to US$0.24 on 8/5/2019).

Bibliography

Birmingham, Walter I. Neustadt and E.N. Omaboe (1966). *A Study of Contemporary Ghana*. Vol 1: The Economy of Ghana, Evanston, IL, Northwestern University Press.

Due, J. (1969). "Agricultural Development in the Ivory Coast and Ghana", *The Journal of Modern African Studies*, Vol. 7, No. 4, pp. 637–660. doi:10.1017/S0022278X00018875 Accessed 7/23/2019.

Fora-Bah, A. and John Asafu-Adjaye (2011). "Scope Economies and Technical Efficiency of Cocoa Agroforestry Systems in Ghana", *Ecological Economics*, Vol. 70, No. 8, June, pp. 1508–1518.

From the London End, Unknown Author (1959). "Ghana's Second Development Plan", *The Economic Weekly Annual*, April 25. www.epw.in/system/files/pdf/1959_11/17/ghana_s_second_development_plan.pdf Accessed 2/25/2019.

Gill & Duffus, (1967). *Cocoa Statistics*, Gill & Duffus Limited, London, England, October.

Government of Ghana (1964). *The Seven-Year Plan for National Reconstruction and Development*, 1963/64–1969/70.

Government of Ghana (2010a). *Medium-Term National Development Policy Framework: Ghana Shared Growth and Development Agenda* (GSGDA), 2010–2013, Government of Ghana, National Development Planning Commission (NDPC), December.

Government of Ghana (2010b). *Medium-Term National Development Policy Framework: Ghana Shared-Growth and Development Agenda* (GSGDA), 2010–2013, Volume 1, Policy Framework, Final Draft, National Development Planning Committee, Accra, September.

Kay, G.B., ed. (1972). *The Political Economy of Colonialism in Ghana: A Collection of Documents and Statistics*, Cambridge, UK, Cambridge University Press.

Kwarteng, Kwame Osei and Edmond Selorm Sosu (2017). "Economic, Social and Political Developments in Ghana: A Relook at the Guggisberg Era in the Gold Coast (1919–1927)", *Historical Research Letter*, Vol. 41, ISSN 2225-0964 (Online), www.iiste.org Accessed 5/14/2019.

Lee, Cassey and Lee Chew-Ging (2017). "The Evolution of Development Planning in Malaysia", *Journal of Southeast Asian Economies*, Vol. 34, No. 3, pp. 436–461.

Lewis, W.A. (1953). *Report on Industrialisation and the Gold Coast*, published, Government Printing Office, Accra.

Miracle, Marvin P. and Ann Seidman (1968). "State Farms in Ghana", University of Wisconsin Land Tenure Center, Madison, March, https://minds.wisconsin.edu/bitstream/handle/1793/36750/340.pdf?sequence=1 Accessed 6/25/2019.

Nuertey, Bernard Narh (1999). *Studies in Oil Palm Based Cropping System in Ghana*, Ph.D. Thesis Submitted to the Board of Graduate Studies, in Partial Fulfilment of the Requirements for the Award of the Degree of Doctor of Philosophy in Crop Science, University of Ghana, Accra, Ghana, October, http://ugspace.ug.edu.gh/bitstream/handle/123456789/7014/Bernard%20Narh%20Nuertey_Studies%20On%20Oil%20Palm%20Based%20Cropping%20Systems%20In%20Ghana_1999.pdf;sequence=1 Accessed 5/14/2019.

Rosenstein-Rodan, P. (1943). "The Problem of Industrialization of Eastern and South-Eastern Europe", *Economic Journal*, Vol. 53, pp. 202–211.

Sachs, Jeffrey and Pia Malaney (2002). "The Economic and Social Burden of Malaria", *Nature*, Vol. 415, No. 6872, February 7, pp. 680–685.

Sundaram, Jomo Kwame and Wee Chong Hui (2014). *Malaysia @50: Economic Development, Distribution, Disparities*, Strategic Information and Development Center, Selangor, Malaysia.

Szereszewski, R. (1965). *Structural Changes in the Economy of Ghana*, Weidenfeld and Nicolson, London, p. 18.

Varatnam, R.V. (1997). *Managing the Malaysian Economy: Challenges and Prospects*, Selangor Darul Ehsan, Malaysia, Pelanduk Publications.

Wessel, Marius and P.M. Foluke Quist Wessel (2015). "Cocoa Production in West Africa, a Review and Analysis of Recent Developments", *NJAS Wageningen, Journal of Life Sciences*, pp. 74–75, 1–7.

Wilks, Ivor and Reviewed Work (2004). "A Woman and a War, Review of '*Yaa Asantewaa and the Asante-British War of 1900-I*'", by A. Adu-Boahen and Emmanuel Akyeampong, in the *Journal of African History*, Vol. 45, No. 2, pp. 324–325, (2 pages), Published by Cambridge University Press.

3 Economic growth and development theories

Introduction: growth and development

Economic growth and economic development are not the same. The two terms are *sometimes* used interchangeably. But even those who do so acknowledge that there is a difference.[1] In Simon Kuznets's Nobel Prize lecture in 1971, he defined economic growth as "a long-term rise in the capacity [of a country] to supply increasingly diverse economic goods to its population". He goes on to further suggest that "this growing capacity [is] based on *advancing technology* and the *institutional* and *ideological adjustments*". Economic growth entails a sustained increase in output over time. This output, referred to as the real gross domestic product (GDP), is the monetary value of all final goods and services produced in an economy over a period, say one year, one quarter, or one month. The real GDP, when divided by the population of the country, gives what is called the real GDP per capita, or what each person in the country will get if the resulting income were divided equally amongst the population. Since the output is never divided equally among the population (some people get less than others), neither the change over time in GDP nor the change over time in per capita GDP accurately captures what economic development really is. Nonetheless, economic growth is essential for economic development. One can liken economic growth to an increase in the size of the pie. The bigger the pie, the bigger the piece each person could get. Economic growth is necessary for economic development; it is, however, not sufficient. Economic development is seen in better health for citizens, increased life expectancy, increased literacy rates and reduced poverty. These outcomes require deliberate policy actions. The more people in the society benefit from economic growth, the more widespread increases in these social welfare indices will be, and the more developed the country will be.

There is no one simple measure of economic development; instead, economists and policy makers use indicators that point to development or the lack of it. Economic development implies the transformation of a society from what it was, to something different, encompassing characteristics that are considered desirable. It is therefore *normative* and may reflect the priorities policy makers or members of the society place on those characteristics. There are some characteristics that many people would agree are desirable, and therefore, society should have more of. Indeed, the more of those characteristics there are, the better the (state of) quality of life. The most often used index is the United Nations Human Development Index (HDI).[2] The HDI is a composite index, calculated using the geometric mean of three-dimension indices: health, education, and income. Because it includes economic and social indicators, it is a better measure of economic development than real GDP per capita.

It is possible for a country to have a relatively high per capita income, and still be classified as less developed. For example, in 2015, the gross national income per capita (purchasing power parity, PPP) of Kuwait was US\$76,075; its HDI was 0.830. On the other hand, the Czech Republic, with a PPP of US\$ 28,144, about a third of Kuwait's, had an HDI of 0.878.

Without growth, improvements in education, medical care, and decent living standards will not be available. Yet, as already stated, human development may still be low even when there is growth. It is up to policy makers to redress imbalances as the economy grows so that the resulting dividend does not disproportionately accrue to a few.

The next section reviews some of the major ideas that economists believe explain economic growth. This will set the stage to examine the extent to which Ghana and Malaysia's growth have conformed to, or failed to conform to, what the theories say. The section also examines in more detail the nexus between growth and development, and tries to shed light on whether policy makers should (1) concentrate on growth in the hope that development will follow naturally or (2) pursue what some have called inclusive growth, reducing inequality while the economy is growing.

Economic growth

A study of the disparity in growth between countries should begin with identifying broadly the factors that promote it in the first place, and how those factors can be manipulated to bring about more of it. While it is agreed that some factors may be more important in one country than another, it is always the case, to paraphrase Domar (1946), that the productive capacity of an economy depends on *factors of production* and the *interplay of economic* and *institutional forces*, such as the distribution of income, consumers' preferences, and the choices policy makers make or do not make.

Growth models are simply the economist's way of trying to explain how and why an economy's capacity to produce goods and services grows over time. The reason for trying to understand the process is simple; to identify the variables that can be controlled so that policy makers could tweak them to influence growth. This is a point Robert M. Solow reiterates in his 1987 Nobel Prize lecture; "growth theory provides a framework within which one can seriously discuss macroeconomic policies that not only achieve and maintain full employment but also make a deliberate choice between current consumption and current investment, and therefore between current consumption and future consumption". The model must not just describe the results of the process generating growth; it must also explain it. It is then that that predictions and policies can flow from the model.

Harrod-Domar model

Early examples of growth models that lent themselves to the twin objectives of understanding the process and being predictive included the Harrod-Domar model. Because the model presented a process that could be understood and used as a policy tool, it was often used or misused for growth policy in developing countries especially, in the 1950s and 1960s when many of the developing countries became independent. One reason was that it is intuitively simple to understand. Second, it did not require too many variables, and finally, it did not require complicated computations. To deploy the model, one begins with the desired rate of growth of the economy ($\Delta Y/Y$), an estimate of the capital-output ratio (K/Y), that is, how many units of capital (K) are required to produce one unit of output (Y). With a constant capital-output ratio, one can readily calculate the savings rate (s) required to achieve the desired growth.[3]

In its simplified version, the rate of growth of the economy is a product of the savings rate (s) and the inverse of capital-output ratio (K/Y). The growth rate resulting from this computation is what is referred to as the warranted growth rate. If the economy grows faster than this warranted rate, it will create an inflationary pressure; if it grows below, it will create a deflationary pressure. For a simplified version, see Appendix I to this chapter.

Empirical evidence over time has shown that differences in investment and capital formation do not explain as much of the differences in economic growth as the Harrod-Domar model predicts. Further, the capital-output ratio is not constant; it changes over time. Also, the model does not make a distinction between skilled and unskilled labor or the role of human capital in the growth process. In spite of these criticisms, the model did provide some useful insights for policy makers and laid the foundation for subsequent models. The emphasis on the role of savings in growth while obvious, had not been formalized in the literature so clearly before. It is still the case that policy makers seeking to increase economic growth need to find ways to increase the savings rate.

The Solow growth model

The Solow growth model can certainly be said to be an extension of the Harrod-Domar model, and it has become the go-to model for understanding how an economy grows. While the major conclusion of the Solow model is that in the long run it is technological progress that increases the per capita income of countries, the transition to that long run still provides some useful policy guidelines.

The model was developed in the 1950s in two seminal articles published in 1956 and 1957. For Solow's contributions to our understanding of economic growth, he was awarded the Nobel Prize in economics. This section discusses, using as few symbols as possible, the major conclusions that are of interest to the project; explaining and accounting for the disparity in growth between Ghana and Malaysia. A brief mathematical version is given in Appendix II. Readers need not understand the mathematical derivation to appreciate the model and its predictions.

An economy produces goods and services using factors of production, inputs, or resources. There are several inputs of production, but let us concentrate on two for now: capital and labor. The relationship between the inputs and the output is called the production function. The more labor and capital the economy has, the more goods and services it can produce. Exactly how much output a country can produce from some given quantities of the inputs depends on the technology the country has. The better the technology, the more output a country can obtain from the inputs. Similarly, a better worker can produce more in a given amount of time with the right equipment. Holding all other factors constant and increasing only one input, the increases in output attributable to the additional factor (the variable input) decreases, diminishing marginal returns. Further, all things remaining constant, a doubling of all inputs will lead to a doubling of output: constant returns to scale. The economy's production function exhibits constant diminishing marginal returns and constant returns to scale.

The most important assumption of the model is that countries, like individuals, can only get rich if they save. In this respect, the Solow model is the same as the Harrod-Domar model. Saving is the postponement of current consumption or the setting aside of some of the current output, gross domestic product (GDP) or income (Y) for other uses, such as replacing or increasing the capital stock. Economists call the act of withholding current output from consumption savings. The savings make it possible to invest (buy new capital equipment or replace worn-out ones). It should be borne in mind that while savings enables the act of investment to take place (i.e., replacing the capital stock and adding to it), those who save and those who invest are not necessarily the same, and the conversion of savings into investment is not a passive act. It requires actors and institutions whose jobs are to bring the savers and investors together.

By replacing and constantly adding to the stock of factors of production, countries can increase their capacity to produce. Naturally, one does not want to devote all output to savings because one has to consume at the present time. The question then is, what is the optimal saving rate. According to the model, the optimal saving rate is the rate that leads to a steady-state where consumption is maximized; this is the "golden rule steady-state". There are many steady states, each corresponding to different saving rates, but only one saving rate yields the steady-state which maximizes consumption, the Golden Rule steady-state.

If a country's saving rate is below *that savings rate*, the golden rule saving rate, it could increase consumption per capita by increasing its saving rate. If the saving rate is above that saving rate, it could increase consumption per capita by reducing the saving rate. In essence, there is no reason for the amount of savings in a country to be such as would maximize consumption per person. It is the task of policy makers to determine if the saving rate is too much or too little, and to pursue policies which will set it right.

Note also that if a country is not at the saving rate that maximizes consumption per person, and policies are enacted to increase the saving rate, consumption per worker will decrease because more of current output is being saved and therefore less is being consumed. The reduction in consumption is temporary, however, since an increase in the saving rate increases the capital per worker, which increases output per worker and thus consumption per worker in the future. In essence, the current generation is postponing consumption so that future generations can consume more; hence, the golden rule steady-state. We would all have liked for our forebears to leave us a larger inheritance of capital stock so that we can produce more per person and consume more per person. If they did not, then the current generation should do what it would have liked the previous generation to do for them; save more now (consume less) so that your children and grandchildren can consume more later.[4] Conversely, if a country has a higher saving rate, it can actually reduce the saving rate to maximize consumption.

Implications of the growth models

Some important conclusions from the Solow model are as follows:

1   For any saving rate, there is a corresponding steady-state at which the capital stock per worker and output per capita are constant;

2 A higher saving rate leads to a greater capital stock per person and a higher output per capita – a new steady-state, where output per worker is higher.
3 There exists a saving rate that leads to a steady-state where the capital per worker and output per worker maximizes consumption; this is the golden rule steady-state.
4 As the economy moves from a lower steady-state to a higher steady-state, capital per worker, output per capita, and consumption per capita increases.
5 At any steady-state, since the capital per worker is constant and output per capita is constant, increases in output per capita are the result of improvements in technology only.

This means that for any country, economic growth can be achieved by *increasing the saving rate* and/or *improving or adopting better technology* to make production more efficient. The constraints to growth then, are *low saving rate* and *inferior technology*. Policy makers must, therefore, pursue policies to encourage savings.

Over time, as the population increases and the number of workers increases, if the additional workers are not equipped with the same capital as workers already in the labor force, capital per worker will decrease, and so will output per worker. If the savings rate does not increase to account for the additional workers, the dilution of the capital per worker will result in output per worker decreasing. The economy could still be growing (GDP will be increasing) but per capita GDP will be decreasing. Therefore, everything else remaining constant, with the same savings rate, countries with *higher population growth* rates will experience lower output per worker.

Further, as workers become more efficient, say through education or on-the-job training, the level of capital they need to produce increases. For example, a worker who has learned how to use a word processor cannot make any impact on output if he or she does not have a word processor. Therefore, to take advantage of this *efficiency*, the savings rate must be high enough to equip the *efficient* (repetitive) worker with additional capital.

The upshot of the preceding discussions means there must be enough savings/investment forthcoming to:

1 Replace worn-out capital (depreciation);
2 Equip new entrants to the labor force (as a result of population growth) with the same amount of capital as workers already in the labor force;
3 Cover the additional demands of increased worker efficiency (e.g., buy computers, etc. for workers capable of using them as a result of education from school or on the job).

Equally important, an economy must find ways to adopt new technology.

The policy prescriptions from the Solow model are richer than what we saw from the Harrod-Domar model. The Harrod-Domar model placed sole emphasis on the savings rate, capital-output being constant. By contrast, the Solow model considers the rate of population growth in conjunction with the savings rate. Having skilled labor, that is, workers who are educated/ trained, makes a difference as well. For a policy maker seeking to increase economic growth, the policy choices are very clear: increase the savings rate, ensure that the rate at which the population grows is not too high, and ensure that workers acquire the skills which will make them productive.

Sources of savings

In a closed economy (an economy that does not interact much with the rest of the world), the total savings for investment must come from within: national savings; the sum of private sector savings from households and businesses; and public sector savings (the difference between government revenue/taxes and expenditure). In an open economy, a third source is available. A country can tap savings from the rest of the world – that is, it can import more from the rest of the world than the rest of the world imports from it. This deficit is actually savings from the rest of the world to the country.

The additional saving from the rest of the world constitutes foreign direct investment (FDI). In order for this additional savings to be forthcoming, a country must create an environment that will be attractive for international businesses to invest, for that is what countries with surplus balances do with their savings. They can use the surplus to acquire domestic businesses already in existence, establish new businesses and/or expand existing foreign-owned businesses in the country (greenfield investment). The conclusions are that

1   Countries that are able to mobilize more domestic savings will grow faster, all things remaining the same;
2   Countries that are more hospitable to foreign direct investment will have more savings from abroad than they are able to mobilize domestically.

Policy makers in both Ghana and Malaysia recognized the importance of savings. Both countries set up institutions designed to mobilize domestic savings and attract foreign investment. Malaysia set up the Permodalan Nasional Berhad (PNB) in the late 1970s to encourage its citizens to save. The PNB convinced Malaysians to purchase share units in its organization, and then used that funds to buy shares in other companies. Ghana similarly set up institutions to finance development. The National Investment Bank (NIB, 1963) was a holdover from the 1963 Ghana Industrial Development Corporation (GIDC), which was itself a holdover from the 1952 Gold Coast Industrial Development Corporation. Unlike Malaysia's PNB, the sources of funds came mostly from the government; very little effort was made to mobilize savings from the public. Consequently, when the government sources dried up, the bank became another universal bank. It was not as able to mobilize domestic savings as PNB.

Big Push theory

There is evidence in both Ghana and Malaysia to suggest that policy makers wittingly or unwittingly pursued policies that are as prescribed by the balanced growth models, of which the most prominent is the *Big Push.*

The Big Push in development economics argues that development cannot proceed in a piecemeal fashion; there must be a concerted effort to launch several complementary projects at the same time. The inertia in an underdeveloped economy requires a big stimulus to overcome. These writings form a part of the ideas contained in *balanced growth theories*, which are also offshoots of the *structuralist approach*; that the rigidities and lags in developing countries are the causes of underdevelopment (see Chenery, 1975). Proponents include Nurkse (1953) and Rosenstein-Rodan (1943, 1961), who argue that poor countries are caught in a "poverty trap". As a general proposition, it is possible for a country to produce less than the potential output because the economy could be trapped in low output equilibrium (Keynesian economics). Such an economy would require a stimulus from outside, such as the government, to get it out of the trap. For poor countries, on the other hand, their inability to get out of the low output equilibrium is the result of several factors which are collectively referred to as indivisibilities. There are indivisibilities in production, demand and savings, and as a result, a big external stimulus or a *big push* is needed to overcome them.

Indivisibilities in production refer to the fact that factors of production, especially capital, tend to be lumpy and cannot be broken down into small pieces. For example, one may not be able to set up a fraction of a utility plant to obtain power for a factory. A lone manufacturing plant that needs the power to operate will find that the cost of constructing such a plant will make its capital-output ratio very high, and therefore the manufacturing process will be inefficient. As more factories move into the area and share in the cost of the utility's cost of operation, each factory will find that its capital-output ratio will decline and its cost of operation will decline as a result. The concept is akin to there being a minimum efficient scale of operation

(MES). There is a minimum output that must be produced to ensure that the unit cost of production is the lowest. Therefore, it might be better to have several factories at once instead of one at a time. This explains why social infrastructure is sometimes difficult to extend to sparsely populated areas of a region. Setting up so many factories at once can be a hefty proposition for many developing countries, which by definition are poor.

In describing indivisibilities in demand, Rosenstein-Rodan used the example of a shoe factory that employs previously unemployed workers. Once employed and drawing income, their expenditure will not only be for the shoes they produce but for other goods and services. It is, therefore, necessary for other factories to be present that can produce the goods and services which workers will demand as a result of their new income. In the absence of these other goods, the shoe factory will not survive.

Both countries, at different times, set up industrial development corporations with the object of coordinating investment in their countries. What is now the Malaysian Investment Development Authority (MIDA) was started as Malaysian Industrial Development Authority in 1967 as a result of the Federal Industrial Development Act of 1965. Its mandate then was to promote investment in the manufacturing and service sectors of the economy. As mentioned elsewhere, Ghana established the Ghana Industrial Development Corporation (GIHOC) to establish state-owned industries because the private sector could not be relied upon to garner the huge investment needed in the country. Malaysia's approach was to encourage foreigners to invest in the local economy through the offering of incentives. The government also mobilized domestic savings to buy shares in foreign companies and in domestic companies.

The lack of loanable funds for investment is also a hindrance. A high volume of investment is required to establish new plants. This high volume, in turn, requires a considerable amount of savings, which are not readily available in poor countries because of low income. The only way to break this vicious cycle is to get a big infusion of income to permit the large volume of savings and investment to take place. These are arguments for the government to play a role in either in the way Malaysia did it and is still doing it, or the way Ghana tried to do it: jump-starting development, as it were. This does not mean that one way or the other is better, but that in order for the government to help, it must have the means to mobilize the savings required.

Institutions

The importance of institutions cannot be overemphasized. Only recently have economists come to realize how important they are for economic development. It is not just financial institutions such as the PNB and NIB.

Economic and political institutions do matter a great deal. Economic growth cannot take place where there is insecurity and/or the absence of institutions to guarantee the gains made by businesses and individuals. Exactly what form these institutions must take is a matter of some debate. The empirical evidence seems quite persuasive. Acemoglu and Robinson (2008) argue that "the main determinants of differences in prosperity across countries are differences in economic institutions". This is not a new idea: Adam Smith (1776) wrote that "Little else is requisite to carry a state to the highest degree of opulence, but peace, easy taxes and tolerable administration of justice: all the rest being brought about by natural course of things". According to Irwin (2014), the tolerable administration of justice requires the establishment of institutions – chief amongst which must be a "legal system to protect private property from encroachment and enforce contracts and the repayment of debt", that is, the presence of a stable government with the essential powers. It is important to remember that Adam Smith did not say that *nothing* else is requisite but, instead, "little else is requisite". While stability does not guarantee development, its absence makes it difficult. A country is more likely to develop if it has a stable government than if it does not. Without stability, planning for the future is difficult and ad hoc, and investors are less likely to invest because of the real or expected risk of losing their assets.

It is therefore not surprising that conflict-prone areas of the world also tend to be poor areas, and poor areas tend to be conflict-ridden; a vicious cycle that can perpetuate poverty. In a background report for the *World Development Report 2018*, Commins (2017) cites fragility, conflict, and violence as obstacles to development. Fragile states are unable to resolve minor conflicts; minor conflicts can lead to or exacerbate violence, which can disrupt and destroy plans and plants.

Because the same government has been in power for decades, Malaysia was able to create Malaysia, despite its tragic ethnic conflicts, has had a generally stable political environment, and has maintained institutions that function effectively and businesses that investors could count on. Ghana, on the other hand, has struggled to maintain political stability. It is not surprising that the longest continuous period of growth in Ghana's history happened since the early 2000s, a period of social and economic stability when the real per capita GDP grew at a sustainable rate of about 4.0% annually.

Appendix I

The Harrod-Domar model: a simplified version

In a closed economy, the demand for GDP (Y), is equal to consumption, C, and investment, I; symbolically:

$$GDP = Y = C + I \qquad\qquad \text{(Eq. 3.1)}$$

Investment is either used to replace worn-out (depreciated) capital stock or to increase it. If depreciation is zero, then all of investment goes to increase the capital stock (K). Investment comes from the savings in the economy, S, thus:

$$S = I = \Delta K \qquad\qquad \text{(Eq. 3.2)}$$

Where ΔK is the change in capital stock.

The capital-output ratio (K/Y) is the amount of capital needed to produce one unit of output or GDP. If it is assumed that K/Y is constant, then in symbols it can be represented by a term α:

$$\frac{K}{Y} = \propto \qquad\qquad \text{(Eq. 3.3)}$$

From equation (3.3)

$$Y = \frac{1}{\alpha} K \qquad\qquad \text{(Eq. 3.4)}$$

Let $\dfrac{1}{\propto} = A$

Then

$$Y = AK \qquad\qquad \text{(Eq. 3.5)}$$

Since A is constant, it is also the case that changes in output are caused only by changes in the capital stock, K, and therefore:

$$\Delta Y = A\Delta K \qquad \text{(Eq. 3.6)}$$

From equation (3.2) we know that savings equal investment, and investment is equal to the change in capital stock. Let S be equal to sY, a fraction of the gross domestic product (GDP), and s is S/Y, the average propensity and the marginal propensity to save or the savings rate.
Then,

$$\Delta K = I = S = sY \qquad \text{(Eq. 3.7)}$$

Combining equations (3.6) and (3.7):

$$\Delta Y = A\Delta K = AsY \qquad \text{(Eq. 3.8)}$$

$$\frac{\Delta Y}{Y} = As = \frac{s}{\propto} \qquad \text{(Eq. 3.9)}$$

Where all terms are as previously defined and α is $1/A$. For policy makers, it is what equation (3.9) enables them to forecast that matters. From equation (3.9) the required savings, s, to reach a growth target of $\Delta Y/Y$ is simply the product of that growth target and the constant $1/A$, as in equation (3.10):

$$s = \frac{\Delta Y}{Y}\alpha \qquad \text{(Eq. 3.10)}$$

If policy makers want a growth rate of 6%, and they know that the capital-output ratio is 4, then from equation (3.10) the savings rate which will generate the 6% growth rate is 24% (6 times 4).

Appendix II

The Solow growth model

The neoclassical growth models, of which the Harrod-Domar and Solow growth models form a part, have greatly influenced how economists now understand the economic growth process. These models use the basic ideas now collectively called classical economics; ideas developed in the 18th and 19th centuries by economists including Adam Smith, Jean-Baptiste Say, and David Ricardo. One of the important tenets stemming from Say's arguments is that an economy will always be at full employment equilibrium. This is now commonly referred to in the literature as Say's Law: "supply creates its own demand". Together with Adam Smith's idea of an *invisible hand* that guides the economy, the classical school held that shortages and surpluses could not persist in the economy. More importantly, there is no need for government intervention. An important criticism of the classical view of how the economy operates was the Keynesian view that while the economy would always tend towards equilibrium, that equilibrium need not necessarily be the full-employment equilibrium. According to Keynes, if an economy were trapped in a low employment equilibrium, there would be no inherent mechanism in the market, absent government intervention, to move it to a higher level of employment and output.

The neoclassical school of thought accepted most of the ideas of the classical school, supply and demand and equilibrium, shortages and surpluses, and causing prices to increase or decrease. What they did not accept was that the economy would always be at full employment. For brevity, we will lump them all together since they all look at growth in more or less the same way and have the same predictive implications. A good representation of neoclassical growth models is the seminal contributions made by Robert M. Solow (1956, 1957). A simplified version of the Solow model will be briefly discussed to highlight some of the important policy variables that economists and policy makers see as critical for economic growth.

In the Keynesian model of the macro economy, a country's gross domestic product or output GDP(Y), is demanded by households (consumption), the government (government expenditure), businesses (investment) and the rest of the world (exports, X). Since the country can also import goods from abroad (M), the net exports (exports less imports) can be positive or negative; that is, a country can consume more than it produces or less than it produces.

Symbolically:

$$Y = C + G + I + X - M \qquad \text{(Eq. 3.11)}$$

Another way of looking at the GDP is to think of it as income generated by households (since they own all the factors of production) and how they dispose of it. Households pay a portion of the income as taxes to the government (T), they consume a portion of what is left (C), the rest is then saved (S). Symbolically:

$$Y = C + T + S \qquad \text{(Eq. 3.12)}$$

Since equations (3.11) and (3.12) are the same (both are measures of the GDP), we can set them equal:

$$Y = C + S + T = C + I + G + X - M \qquad \text{(Eq. 3.13)}$$

And solve for *I*, investment as

$$I = S + (T - G) + (M - X) \qquad \text{(Eq. 3.14)}$$

On the right-hand side, S is private sector savings, $T - G$ is public sector or government savings, and $M - X$ is savings by the rest of the world, or net exports, which can be positive or negative depending on whether exports are greater or less than imports. The private sector and government savings constitute national savings.

We can collapse equation (3.14) into the well-known Keynesian equilibrium condition:

$$I = S \qquad \text{(Eq. 3.15)}$$

or savings equals investment ($S = I$). All investment comes from savings, and savings can be domestic or borrowed. This important relationship also underlies all the neoclassical growth models. First, investment comes from savings. Second, savings come from foregone consumption by the private and public sectors. Finally, a country that does not save enough to make the desired or required amount of investment can borrow from abroad.

Investment and capital

Economic growth depends on the availability of factors of production and how productive the factors are or the state of technology. The factors of production include labor, natural resources (land and all that is in it) and physical capital (machinery, etc.). For now, we can treat natural resources as fixed and focus on the factors that appear to explain growth in most countries. This does not mean that natural resources are not important. The high levels of income enjoyed by countries such as the United States are due in part to the abundant natural resources they have: fertile land, oil, timber, long and wide rivers which flow through the length and breadth of the country, and so forth. On the other hand, countries such as Japan, South Korea, and Taiwan have demonstrated that while natural resources are important, their absence does not necessarily mean the absence of development. Indeed, many countries with abundant resources suffer from what is known as the "resource curse" (Auty, 1993), the condition where abundant resources lead to slower economic growth. Sachs and Warner (1995), in an NBER paper, concluded that "economies with high natural-resource exports to GDP ratio, tended to have less growth rates" in the period 1971 to 1989. This could be the result of less local processing and hence less multiplier effects.

In symbols,

$$Y = F(K, L * E, H) \qquad \text{(Eq. 3.16)}$$

where
Y is output or real GDP
K is capital stock
L is labor
E and H is human capital.

For ease of discussions, let us for now, ignore human capital, H and E, the efficiency of labor. The common practice is to convert the production function into per capita terms. This can be done if it is assumed that the production function exhibits constant returns to scale. Dividing all the factors by L, the amount of labor gives us:

$$\frac{Y}{L} = F\left(\frac{K}{L}, \frac{L}{L}\right) \qquad \text{(Eq. 3.17)}$$

where
Y/L, y is output per worker
K/L, k, is capital per worker and
L/L, 1, does not feature into the dynamics of the equation.

Equation (3.17) says that the output per capita depends on the capital stock per worker or the capital-labor ratio.

$$y = f(k) \tag{Eq. 3.18}$$

Now, let us assume that each worker saves s, a constant fraction of income. Savings per worker is then:

$$sy = sf(k) \tag{Eq. 3.19}$$

We have already shown in equation (13.5) that savings equal investment ($I = S$). In per capita terms, investment per worker is, therefore, equal to savings per worker.

$$i = sy = sf(k) \tag{Eq. 3.20}$$

The total savings per worker in the economy, which is equal to the investment per worker, is used to replace depreciated capital stock per worker, δk, and to increase the capital stock per worker, Δk.
    So,

$$sy = sf(k) = i = \delta k + \Delta k \tag{Eq. 3.21}$$

The change in capital stock ($\Delta k = sf(k) - \delta k$) is the difference between the totals savings per worker $sf(k)$ and the depreciation of capital stock per worker, δk. If Δk is positive, capital stock per worker increases over time, and since output per worker depends positively on capital per worker, output per worker also grows. Conversely, if Δk is negative, the capital stock decreases, and output per worker also decreases. Finally, if $\Delta k = 0$, then capital stock per worker does not change, it is constant and so is output per worker. When this happens, the economy is said to be in a *steady state*.
    In the steady state, output per capita does not grow because capital stock per worker does not grow. Total output, however, does grow. Since the goal of economic policy is to increase the standard of living, simply increasing output will not suffice.

The assumptions that lead the discussions should be borne in mind.

1   The rate at which capital per worker depreciates (δ) is constant;
2   The production function exhibits diminishing marginal returns;
3   The production function exhibits constant returns to scale.

The first step in making predictions from the model is to solve for k. To do so, let us use a Cobb-Douglas production function of the following specific form:

$$Y = K^{\alpha} L^{1-\alpha}$$

where
Y is the output
K is capital stock
L is labor stock, and α and $1 - \alpha$ are the output elasticities of capital and labor, respectively.

In a Cobb-Douglas production function, the sum of the output elasticities equal one; the production function exhibits constant returns to scale.

If we convert all sides to per capita terms (by dividing by labor, L), we get

$$y = k^{\alpha}$$

Saving per worker is $sy = sk^{\alpha} = i = \delta k + \Delta k$
In the steady $\Delta k = 0$ and thus

$$sk^{\alpha} = \delta k$$

The steady-state capital stock $k*$ is, therefore:

$$k* = \left(\frac{s}{\delta} \right)^{1/(1-\alpha)} \tag{Eq. 3.22}$$

As shown in equation (3.22), the steady-state capital stock depends on the saving rate (s) and the depreciation rate (δ). All things equal, an increase in the saving rate leads to an increase in the steady-state capital stock and hence, an increase in output per worker. On the other hand, an increase in the rate at which capital stock depreciates leads to a decline in the steady-state capital stock per worker and in output per worker. The upshot is that countries that seek to grow should increase the savings rate.

Without belaboring the discussion too much, as a country's population grows, so will the number of workers. Since total output increases at a diminishing rate with the number of workers, total output will increase. What happens to output per worker, however, depends on whether each new worker has the same, more, or less capital stock as the previous workers. To maintain the same output per worker, each new worker must be equipped with as much capital as earlier workers. In effect, as the population increases, unless the saving rate increases to add new capital stock for new entrants to the labor market, capital stock per worker will decline, and output per worker will decrease.

Equation 3.22 can be reworked to include the population growth, n; which enters the equation in the same way as the depreciation rate. In this case, when investment per worker, i, is exactly equal to the depreciation rate (δ) and population growth (n); the economy is in a steady-state; is $sy = sk^{\alpha} = i = \delta k + nk + \Delta k$. In the steady state, $\Delta k = 0$, and thus $i = sy = sk^{\alpha} = \delta k + nk$.

Solving for the steady-state capital stock produces:

$$k^* = \left(\frac{s}{(\delta + n)} \right)^{1/(1-\alpha)}$$
(Eq. 3.23)

Given s, the savings rate, an increase in δ or n dilutes the steady-state capital stock, and the output per worker.

Improvements in human capital can be thought of as an increase in the labor force. It is like the case where a worker has become more productive because of new skills acquired, and thus needs better equipment capital than before; a computer instead of a typewriter, a tractor instead of a hoe or machete. This means that the savings rate must increase to accommodate the additional capital stock for the more productive or skilled worker. This can be thought of as an improvement in technology through labor or labor augmenting technological progress. The rate of labor augmenting technical progress can be included in the equation as g, in the denominator. As can be seen in equation 3.24, increases in labor, n, in depreciation δ, and improvement in technology, g, dilute the steady-state capital stock. In order to keep the capital stock constant, the saving rate must therefore increase.

$$k^* = \left(\frac{s}{(\delta + n + g)} \right)^{1/(1-\alpha)}$$
(Eq. 3.24)

Technology

In the Solow model, technology is exogenous. However, citing Wolf (1987), Solow (1987) also argues that technological progress could find its way into production with the adoption of new and different capital equipment. This means that as a country saves and invests more, and increases its capital-output ratio, it also benefits from the improved technology embodied in the higher capital-output per worker. Technology, therefore, comes as a side effect of a larger output. This could explain why as countries grow, the level of technology also advances. The higher the GDP, the more resources a country can devote to basic research and development (R&D), the sources of technological improvement. According to Baumol (2002), innovation is the most competitive weapon and the main driver of economic growth in a capitalist economy. Because of its importance in the competitive market, large firms have made innovation a routine part of their operation. In a sense, this has become a virtuous cycle; large firms in developed economies devote a large share of resources to R&D. The resulting improvement in technology leads to greater output, which enables them to devote more to R&D, and on and on it goes.

This means that poor countries could find themselves perpetually lagging behind developed economies in growth unless they can somehow find a way to obtain the technology without the initial expenditure required to generate it. This is not so easy; the protection of intellectual property rights is one of the bedrocks of international trade.[5] In the same developed countries, in addition to large firms devoting large resources to and routinizing R&D, governments also support basic and applied research with large grants. For example, between 2000 and 2015, gross domestic expenditure on R&D by businesses, higher education institutions, and private and non-profit enterprises on basic and applied research and experimental development, as a percent of GDP in the OECD countries, was 2.33%. Many developing countries cannot devote such a large percentage of their GDP to the pursuit of research.[6]

Implications

The essence of the neoclassical growth models, of which the Solow model is a good representation, is that economic growth proceeds from increases in the capital stock and improvements in technology. Since capital stock depends on investment and investment itself is the result of savings, one can conclude that savings is critical for the wealth of nations.

Notes

1 Van Den Berg, Hendrik, *Economic Growth and Development*, 3rd Edition, McGraw-Hill, 2016. (Stewart, 2018).
2 http://hdr.undp.org/sites/default/files/hdr2016_technical_notes.pdf, accessed 6/12/2018.

3 For an explication of the Harrod and Domar models, see Ezeala-Harrison, Fidelis, *Economic Development: Theory and Policy Application*, Westport, CT, USA, Praeger, 1996, pp. 96–99.
4 Matthew 22:39. The English Standard Version gives it as follows "And a second is like it: You shall love your neighbor as yourself".
5 www.wto.org/english/tratop_e/trips_e/intel1_e.htm, accessed 10/22/2018.
6 www.sciencemag.org/news/2017/03/data-check-us-government-share-basic-research-funding-falls-below-50, accessed 10/10/2018.
www.worldbank.org/en/topic/fragilityconflictviolence/overview, accessed 10/22/2018.

Bibliography

Acemoglu, Daron and James A. Robinson (2008). "The Role of Institutions in Economic Growth and Development", Background Paper for Commission on Growth and Development, Working Paper No. 10, World Bank, Washington, DC.

Auty, Richard M. (1990). *Resource-Based Industrialization: Sowing the Oil in Eight Developing Countries*, New York, Oxford University Press.

Auty, Richard M. (1993). *Sustaining Development in Mineral Economies: The Resource Curse Thesis*, London and New York, Routledge.

Baumol, William J. (2002). *The Free-Market Innovation Machine: Analyzing the Growth Miracle of Capitalism*, Princeton, Princeton University Press.

Chenery, Hollis B. (1975). "The Structuralist Approach to Development Policy", *American Economic Review*, Vol. 65.

Commins, Stephen (2017). "Fragility, Conflict, and Violence", Background Report: Learning to Realize Education's Promise World Development Report 2018, World Bank, Washington, DC, www.dartmouth.edu/~dirwin/docs/w20636.pdf Accessed 7/15/2019.

Domar, Evsey (1946). "Capital Expansion, Rate of Growth and Employment", *Econometric*, Vol. 14, No. 2, April, pp. 137–147.

Dugald, Stewart (1793). "Account of the Life and Writings of Adam Smith", *The Works of Dugald Stewart*, in Seven Volumes, Vol. 8, p. 64, Cambridge, Published by Hilliard and Brown in 1829.

Harrod, Roy F. (1939). "An Essay in Dynamic Theory", *The Economic Journal*, Vol. 49, No. 193, March, pp. 14–33.

Irwin, Douglas and Adam Smith (2014). "Tolerable Administration of Justice and the Wealth of Nations", NBER Working Paper 20636, Cambridge, MA, www.nber.org/papers/w20636 Accessed 6/14/2018.

Nurkse, Ragner (1953). *Problems of Capital Formation in Underdeveloped Countries*, Oxford, Oxford University Press.

Romer, P.M. (1994). "The Origins of Endogenous Growth", *The Journal of Economic Perspectives*, Vol. 8, No. 1, pp. 3–22.

Rosenstein-Rodan, Paul N. (1943). "Problems of Industrialization in Eastern and Southeastern Europe", *Economic Journal*, Vol. 53.

Rosenstein-Rodan, Paul N. (1961). "Notes on the Theory of the 'Big Push'", in *Economic Development for Latin America*, edited by H.S. Elis and H.C. Wallich, London, Macmillan.

Sachs, Jeffrey D. and Andrew M. Warner (1995). "Natural Resource Abundance and Economic Growth", NBER Working Paper Series # 5398, Cambridge, MA.

Solow, Robert M. (1956). "A Contribution to the Theory of Economic Growth", *Quarterly Journal of Economics*, Vol. 70, February, pp. 65–94.

Solow, Robert M. (1957). "Technical Change and the Aggregate Production Function", *Review of Economics and Statistics*, Vol. 39, August, pp. 312–320.

Solow, Robert M. (1987). "Nobel Prize Lecture, Lecture to the memory of Alfred Nobel", December 8, p. 1, Sweden. Full Speech can be accessed as of 1/9/2020 at http://citeseerx.ist.psu.edu/viewdoc/download?doi=10.1.1.645.164&rep=rep1&type=pdf

Waterman, A.M.C. (2011). "Neoclassical and Classical Growth Theory Compared", St John's College, Winnipeg R3T 2M5, Canada, https://amcwaterman.files.wordpress.com/2011/05/neoclassical-classical-growth.doc Accessed 6/27/2018.

Wolff, E. (1987). "Capital Formation and Long-Term Productivity Growth", *Working Paper*, C.V. Starr Center for Applied Economics, New York University, September.

4 Determinants of economic growth in Ghana

Survey of the literature

Introduction

In Chapter 3, we reviewed some of the basic theories of economic growth. In this chapter, we survey the literature on the determinants of economic growth in Ghana with a view to identifying the specific ones that may have enhanced or inhibited growth. There are several academic works that have focused on the determinants of economic growth in Ghana. In this chapter we review a few of the studies.

Growth strategy

From independence, it was the plan of the new government to industrialize as quickly as possible and to do so using Ghanaian resources, both human and natural; it had plenty of the latter but not the former. The first attempts at industrialization involved the familiar import substitution industrialization (ISI). Between 1965 and 1983, several factories were established to produce consumer goods in order to reduce imports and to develop the base for manufacturing. To ensure that the factories succeeded, import restrictions were introduced and foreign exchange controls imposed. While the factories were set up to use local inputs, the supply chain had not been properly developed; it was not dependable and many of the factories found themselves with excess capacity. Most of the factories were set up to process agricultural products such as rice, copra, tomatoes and beef. This made a lot of sense, since Ghana was primarily an agricultural country. Unfortunately, the local supply of the raw materials proved to be unpredictable and together with the difficulty of obtaining foreign currency to import the raw materials, for the most part, the factories could not produce enough to meet local demand. In any event, the next stage of industrialization, exports of industrial goods, never materialized. By the time the economy became liberalized in in the 1980s, many of the factories were obsolete and the state enterprises that still remained were operating at losses. This was a clear case of the government choosing winners and losing. The industrial policy (ISI) itself was not the problem; it was the implementation. In many countries where ISI has been implemented successfully, the government has not done it alone. Instead, the government cajoled the private sector, created conditions for foreign direct investment (e.g. developing infrastructure, providing good quality education make skilled workers available), and provided efficient institutions. Inability to do these resulted in Ghana losing the advantage it had at independence, when it was touted as having the best infrastructure in the region and the best chance to become developed.

Growth in the 2010s has been quite impressive, averaging 4.4%. This is no doubt the result of social and political stability, the discovery of commercial quantities of oil in 2007 and the adoption of liberal economic policies that has led to a comparatively large steady inflow of FDI, averaging 7.08% of GDP between 2007 and 2017. For the rest of the chapter, we look at some at some of the factors that prevented Ghana from realizing its potential in the 60 or so years after independence.

The factors of production

In Chapter 3, we saw the importance of the various factors of production that growth theory suggest will increase output per person. Labor and capital are very important in the production process. Equally important are the complementary factors; the skill and health of the workers, the capital each worker has to work with and the environment in which they work. These complementary factors, which make workers more productive, require savings; from the domestic economy or from abroad. Finally, the absence of natural resources is not necessarily an obstacle to economic growth.

Natural resources

Ghana is well endowed with natural resources, from its tropical forest filled with hard and soft wood to rare minerals like gold, manganese, bauxite and diamonds. Unlike other African countries that are landlocked, Ghana has an Atlantic coastline that is 334 miles (537.5 kilometers) long and not too far from the developed countries of Europe and the United States. Its tropical climate and fertile land has enabled it to produce enough cocoa to become a leading supplier to the world. It could also produce rubber, oil palm, rice, sisal and many tropical agricultural products. Its arable land, 20.66% of the total land area of 92,497 square miles (239,566 square kilometers) is believed by the World Bank to have the potential to be a leading sector of the economy that could be "the engine of job creation and economic growth".[1] The poor economic performance is the result of wrong policies or correct ones not pursued properly; more likely, both. Its long interaction with the British left it with a sound economic structure, an infrastructure that was then quite ahead of its many neighbors, and a per capita GDP that was low but higher than many developing countries at that time. Ghana may have sought to develop rapidly after independence, but it could have probably have gone further by *making haste slowly.*

Among some of the factors that have probably prevented agriculture from playing the role of a leading sector is the system of land tenure and the inability of government policy to apply the same method it used to make cocoa a leading sector to other crops.

Land tenure and agriculture

Growth theories often take certain institutions as given and assume that they will not be obstacles. For example, while one might discuss agricultural productivity in the context of land fertility, there are more obstacles that make the mere presence of fertile land unproductive. Land is a factor of production and despite its immovable nature, it can be quite fungible (i.e., it can be exchanged in whole or in part for something else, if the land tenure system allows it). In his 2000 book *The Mystery of Capital*, De Soto argues that there is a lot of capital locked up in land in the developing countries, which if unleashed, could go a long way towards helping in economic development. The inability to tap the capital locked in land, he argues, is due to the nature property rights or lack of property rights.

It will be recalled that in Arthur Lewis's Report to the Gold Coast Government in the early 1950s, he had emphasized the importance of increasing productivity in agriculture so that fewer workers would be needed in the sector and the surplus could move into industry. He saw the increased productivity not only releasing labor, but also providing additional revenue for development.[2]

Quraishy (1971) attributes the low productivity in agriculture in Ghana to the system of land tenure. Access to land in the traditional society still favors men over women even though a large number of women in the rural areas are in agriculture. The land tenure system is not easy to navigate. In the southern part of Ghana, land either belongs to the family and is overseen by the head of the family or, it belongs to the community and is vested in the *nana* (king) or the stool.[3] It is often not easy to determine who "owns" the land at any one time since different people may have different rights in the land. In such a situation, lenders are reluctant to accept land as collateral for loans. Further, because of the difficulty in determining ownership or the proper person to alienate the land (buy from), there are often intra-family squabbles, multiple sales and claims to ownership that result in the courts being inundated with land cases.[4] Equity in land, from which many in the west draw for business ventures, is virtually absent in Ghana.[5] The conclusion is that the land tenure system as it exists now in Ghana is not a positive factor in economic development. The enclosure movement in the 1700s in England, which launched the agricultural revolution and the industrial revolution, essentially allowed common land areas to become privately owned. Not so in Ghana: Land is still for the most part communally held. When one only possesses land, and does not own it, the incentive to improve it is not as great. Not improving land (digging wells to store water, building canals to bring water, ensuring proper drainage and erecting walls to prevent encroachment) leads to low yields. This, in part, explains the low productivity found in the sector. Improving the land tenure system then should help.

Population growth, labor, and human capital

The rate at which the population grows can be a significant factor in increasing or decreasing per capita economic growth. It is true that a bigger population provides a bigger market for domestic industries and also provides a large supply of labor and presumably a large pool of thinkers and inventors.[6] But a bigger population can also dilute the rate at which per capita GDP grows. Moreover, a large population does not mean a skilled labor force. There must be an investment in the population to make it healthy and skilled, and this requires a deliberate policy to allocate funds to these efforts. It is the skilled labor that has the technical and managerial abilities to plan, execute or monitor a piece of task or project. Such skills can be acquired on the job or in formal educational settings. At independence, Ghana, unlike Malaysia, sought to indigenize its economy immediately, and therefore encouraged colonial expatriates to depart. Although the British council and the US government did subsequently send in lots of teachers, especially during the 1960s and 1970s, the departure of so many skilled workers at one time could not but negatively affect growth for a long time. An economy not only needs skilled workers, but healthy skilled workers. A government that spends to educate its population and ensures that they are healthy will see the benefits in terms of increased productivity and high economic growth rates. A study by King, Glewwe and Alberts (1992) suggests that the lack of good primary and secondary education, and the poor health of workers, negatively affected growth in Ghana. In their recommendations, they suggest that the government assign priority to improving the health of the population through primary and preventative health care. Several other studies have come to the same conclusion. Alhassan, Donkoh and Asante (2012), in a study covering 1960 to 2007, note that while many more people were enrolled in education during the period, the quality still needed to be improved in order for education to have a positive impact on economic growth. In a study by Adu (2013) covering the period 1961 to 2009, he concludes that the key determinants of economic growth in Ghana include the labor force. Adu's study finds that the coefficient of labor was positive and had an elasticity closer to one than found by other studies. As Adu points out, this large coefficient is inconsistent with many studies of the genre, which peg the coefficient at between one-third and two-thirds. On the other hand, if one accepts this large labor coefficient, then it helps to explain the poor performance of the Ghanaian economy in the 1970s and 1980s, when many in the labor force (skilled and unskilled) left for Nigeria. Education is what makes labor skilled and productive. In a study by Raggl (2014) covering the period 1970–2009, however, he concluded that education was not a significant factor in determining economic growth. This finding is at odds with conventional wisdom and with other studies. Most labor economists argue that education increases human capital and thus labor productivity. It may very well be that even though many people are going to school, as pointed out earlier, the quality of education is poor and is therefore not imparting much skill into labor. Anaman (2006) comes to the same conclusion regarding labor, observing that labor productivity was very low and did not contribute much to growth. He suggests that it may be due to the absence of complementary factors. On the other hand, a study by Ho and Iyke (2018) concludes that in the long run, human capital had a positive effect on growth but labor had a short-run negative effect.

Taken together, the studies suggest there is low labor productivity in Ghana and that it may be due to the absence of complementary factors, the low quality of education, and the poor health of workers.

Savings, investment, and capital

The complementary factors which labor needs to be productive include tools and modern technology. In the cocoa sector, for example, farmers have traditionally used simple tools such as machetes but have been able to produce large quantities of the crop using help from extension services which provided advice. In addition, the government has invested in the development of higher yielding seedlings as well as encouraging the use of fertilizers. The same cannot be said of other crops. The new technology and capital needed to increase productivity must come from savings, domestic or foreign. Havi et al. (2013) looked at the determinants of economic growth in

Ghana between 1970 and 2011 and concluded that in the long run, physical capital and foreign direct investment had positive effects on real per capita GDP growth. This is not surprising, because in a country with a large labor supply and very little capital, the marginal product of the latter should be high. In the same study, they concluded that foreign aid had a negative long-run impact. The study however, also concluded that in the short run, FDI had a negative impact. A plausible explanation might be that FDI has a long gestation period and foreign investors like to get their returns as quickly as possible, and hence the returns to the domestic economy comes much later. Yet another study on the factors affecting growth in Ghana by Antwi, Mills and Zhao (2013) using data from 1980 to 2010 concluded that while physical capital had positive effects on per capita GDP, FDI had a negative effect on real GDP per capita. Iyke (2014), using an augmented Solow growth model, examined human capital, physical capital, labor, government expenditure, inflation, foreign aid, foreign direct investment, financial development, globalization, and debt servicing on Ghana's economic performance. The conclusions of the paper are that in the long run, human capital and foreign aid have positive effects on economic growth while labor, financial development and debt servicing have a negative impact. In the short run, government expenditure and foreign aid have positive impacts but labor, inflation and financial development have negative impacts.

Macroeconomic environment

The macroeconomic environment can be an inhibiting factor in economic growth. While a mild inflation in the economy is not necessarily bad, high and variable inflation is not good in the sense that it distorts the signals sent by price to producers and consumers alike. In a review of the Ghanaian economy from 1970 to 2009, Herrera and Aykut (2014) found that inflation and government spending were negatively associated with growth. In a study covering the period 1960 to 2007, Alhassan, Donkoh and Asante (2012) identify financial and political instability, inflation, increases in government consumption, and debt as having negative impacts on economic growth, in a study covering the period from 1960 to 2007. Government spending, especially if it requires monetizing the deficit, as in selling treasuries to the central bank, creates inflation. Inflation, if it is high, decreases the purchasing power of money. Such was the case in Ghana in the 1980s to the mid-2000s. Prices were being quoted in millions of the domestic currency (cedis). In a cash economy as Ghana is still, and with currency denominated in small units, logging money around became a burden and safety hazard. Conducting transactions in the local currency entailed carrying large sums of small denomination currencies, which meant additional costs in security and storage. Businesses had to invest in counting machines. People began to substitute other currencies for the cedi. Long-term contracts and prices were being quoted in US dollars; it was not unusual, in the cities, to hear people holding dollars as stores of value instead of the cedis. The high rate of inflation led the Bank of Ghana to eventually redenominate the currency in 2007; dividing it by 10,000. The reasons stated were that the diminished value of the currency made it "difficult to maintain accounting and statistical records" as well as data processing.[7] These macroeconomic developments did not happen overnight; they began almost as early as the late 1970s and continued well into the 1990s. The reasons for the high inflation was inadequate government revenue and the resulting deficit financing or monetary expansion. From 1965 to 2018, the average inflation rate was 27.91 percent with a standard deviation of 27. Not only was inflation high, it was also volatile. Between 1971 and 1981, the average rate of price increase was 50.17%, reaching a high of 122.87% in 1983. An inflation rate of 50% is classified as hyperinflationary; thus the country was experiencing hyperinflation. As Table 4.1 shows, inflation has been tapering off, but it is still high.

The high and variable inflation leads to uncertainty and more importantly, in the case of Ghana, to negative interest rates for savers and high lending rates for borrowers; the first discourages domestic savings, and the second discourages investment, neither of which is good for economic growth. Table 4.2 shows the real interest rates on government securities and savings deposits for the 2000s when the economy had stabilized some. Even so, for most of the period, the real interest rate on savings deposits was negative.

It is easy to blame the structural adjustment program (SAP) introduced by the World Bank as part of the cause of the difficulties Ghana had. It should be borne in mind that SAP began in the 1980s, when the economy was already in a free fall. Second, SAP was intended to stabilize and rectify the decline in growth. If the economy had been in good shape, there would have been no need for SAP.

Table 4.1 Inflation in Ghana

Period	Inflation (%)
1971–1981	50.17
1982–2000	32.50
2001–2007	17.68
2008–2017	13.30
1965–2018	27.91

Source: World Bank, www.macrotrends.net, accessed 11/21/2019.

Table 4.2 Interest rates in Ghana

Year	Inflation	Nominal Interest Rate: Annual		Real Interest Rate: Annual	
		Govt. Securities	Savings Deposits	Govt. Securities	Savings Deposits
2004	12.62	21.20	8.35	8.58	−4.27
2005	15.12	20.54	6.13	5.42	−8.99
2006	10.92	16.42	4.65	5.50	−6.27
2007	10.73	12.71	5.80	1.98	−4.93
2008	16.52	14.89	9.17	−1.63	−7.35
2009	19.25	16.00	7.92	−3.25	−11.33
2010	10.71	15.14	5.18	4.43	−5.53
2011	8.73	13.43	4.86	4.70	−3.87
2012	7.13	20.41	5.35	13.28	−1.78
2013	11.67	18.24	5.44	6.57	−6.23
2014	15.49	24.34	6.09	8.85	−9.40

Sources: World Bank: www.macrotrends.net; International Financial Statistics (IFS).

Open or closed economy

For some time in the 1960s to the 1970s, the Ghanaian economy was virtually a closed economy. This was during the period when the government was pursuing ISI. Import and exchange controls were instituted to boost domestic production of consumer goods. This virtual closure of the economy did not do much to help growth. In a review of the Ghanaian economy from 1970 to 2009, Aykut (2014) found that trade openness and had a positive impact on economic growth. The general consensus among economists is that free trade promotes growth. Mankiw (p. 255), citing from Sachs and Warner (1995), indicates that between 1970 and 1989. Developing economies that were closed grew at 0.7% a year (same as the developed economies that were closed). On the other hand, developing countries that were open grew at 4.5% a year.[8] Ghana did a little better during the period, real GDP grew at 1.72% during the period; real GDP per capita, however, grew at −0.90%. It may be coincidental or it may not, but since the 1990s, when the economy became open, growth has been better. While initial comparative advantage may consign a developing country to producing agricultural goods, there is a natural progression from producing those goods efficiently to processing them to add more value for local consumers and then for a wider market. The case of Malaysia and oil palm is a good example.

Political and social stability, institutions, and corruption

Anaman (2006) looked at the factors that affected long-run growth in Ghana over the period 1957 to 2005 and came to the conclusion that political instability was a significant negative factor. The same conclusion is arrived at by Alhassan, Donkoh and Asante (2012). Between 1966 and 1981 there were five successful coups d'état and one failed attempt in the country. In between, there several attempts at changing the government that did not rise to the surface. The military regimes that emerged from the changes in government tended to be full of idealist who had no sense of what it took to run a country. The civilian governments that succeeded the military governments were not given enough time to get settled before another overthrow of government took place. In the circumstances, the economy was, as it were, adrift, with no well-thought-out sense of direction. There was a general belief among the soldiers, in particular, that all that was needed was to get rid of a few corrupt people and everything was going to be all right. The problem was not that simple; it was the bureaucracy, the institutions, and the pervasive corruption that had become embedded in the system.

Ahmad, Ullah and Arfeen (2012) in a study titled "Does Corruption Affect Economic Growth?" concluded that indeed it does, though not in the linear way often assumed. The study shows that corruption, bureaucratic inefficiency, political instability, and institutional inefficiency significantly reduce GDP per worker. Corruption, in addition to reducing the marginal product of labor, also negatively affects GDP growth through decreasing domestic and foreign direct investment, encouraging excessive government expenditure, distorting the allocation of government expenditure away from education, health, and the maintenance of infrastructure towards less efficient public projects that provide more scope for manipulation, bribe-taking opportunities and nepotism. Weak institutions, bureaucratic inefficiencies and political instability all likewise negatively affect growth. All these were true in Ghana and intensified in the 1980s.

The Ghanaian Center for Democratic Development estimates that corruption cost the country close to US$2 billion in three years – and that, it says, is an underestimation.[9] Corruption is not benign; it increases the cost of doing business in the country and frustrates both consumers and businesses. Ofori et al. (2015) in a study of the Ghanaian economy from 2004 to 2014, suggest that corruption does indeed reduce the inflow of FDI. They also indicate that corruption reduces the revenue that should go to the government for development and directly hurts small and medium enterprises (SMEs) because, unlike bigger enterprises, they do not have the means to fight corruption. Since the SMEs employ about 85% of people in the manufacturing sector and contribute significantly to GDP, this means that if the additional costs imposed by corruption were removed, they could do more to contribute to growth.

Summary and conclusions

In a piece by Leite et al. (2000) covering the period 1992 to 1999, the authors highlight most of the basic findings outlined in the articles reviewed earlier. To a large extent, the critical factors detracting from rapid growth in Ghana have not changed much since they were diagnosed in the 1960s and before. Guggisberg and Lewis both indicated the need to increase productivity in the agricultural sector and diversify the export base away from a few crops. While Ghana is basically an agricultural country, the entire economy depends mainly on the production and export of cocoa, some minerals, and, since 2007, oil. It also produces grains for domestic consumption, but has had to import large quantities of cereal from abroad. After years of planning and trying to diversify the agricultural sector, it is still not sufficiently diversified to withstand fluctuations in the prices of the few commodities that it exports. Fluctuations in the prices of cocoa and gold still cause problems. The recent good performance of the economy is the result of the relatively high price of gold and the recent discovery of oil (albeit at a time when oil prices are not as high as they used to be in the late 1970s and early 1980s).

The agriculture production chain is not efficient; there is very low use of technology along the value chain. The low use of technology leads to a large percentage of post-harvest losses (PHL).[10] Minimizing losses in harvesting, assembling, shelling, storing, milling, packaging, transporting, and marketing could make a substantial difference in incomes received along the supply chain, reduce imports, and increase exports.

Several of the studies suggest that low labor productivity could be attributed to the low quality of education and the poor health of workers. While many more boys and girls are now enrolled in schools, very few of them will have the opportunity to proceed beyond the primary level. A clear case of misallocation government expenditure lies in the fact that while expenditure per pupil is higher in the tertiary educational system, many graduates from the sector are now struggling to find employment. Many college graduates troll the streets for months and years before finding jobs or settling for jobs that demand fewer capabilities than they have acquired. Since many people will not go to the university, a good elementary education (K–12) could go a long way towards improving labor productivity. These are structural impediments which have to be addressed in order for the country to attain long-term sustainable growth.

The macroeconomic environment has gotten better since the mid-2000s but still has a long way to go. Interest rates on borrowing are still very high

For example, the commercial bank lending rate as of June 2019 was 27.68% and saving deposits earned 7.55%.[11] At the same time, inflation was 9.1%.[12] This means that the real interest rate on commercial bank loans was 18.58% and savers were losing money (−1.55% for savings deposits). This discourages savings and borrowing.

Privatizing some sectors of the economy has no doubt boosted productivity in ways that are not easily measurable but nonetheless visible. The presence of private companies such as Vodaphone has transformed telecommunication in the country and no doubt increased productivity. There are sectors which the government still controls, but which could be efficiently performed by the private sector.

Notes

1 www.worldatlas.com/articles/what-are-the-major-natural-resources-of-ghana. html, accessed 9/10/2019.
2 Revenue from cocoa taxes have done this for Ghana.
3 The stool is the traditional symbol for kingship or chieftaincy. It is literally a chair, equivalent to a throne.
4 See Kline, Aimee, Élan Moore, Elizabeth Ramey, Kevin Hernandez, Lauren Ehrhardt, Megan Reed, Morgan Parker, Samantha Henson, Taylor Winn and Taylor Wood, "Whose Land Is It Anyway? Navigating Ghana's Complex Land System", *Texas A&M Law Review*, Vol. 6, No. 1 (January 2019), Article 15.
5 See Andoh and Gebremariam, "Property Rights, Capital Accumulation and Economic Development: The Case of Ghana", *Intercultural Management Quarterly*, Vol. 11, No. 1 (Winter 2010), pp. 17–19.
6 Kremer, Michael, "Population Growth and Technological Change: One Million BC to 1990", *Quarterly Journal of Economics*, Vol. 108 (August 1993), pp. 681–716. One may disagree with some of the inferences but intuitively, a larger population could be a spur to growth, if from nothing, then from the inevitable struggle to survive from the large population itself.
7 Source: www.pwc.com/gh/en/publications/redenomination-of-the-cedi.html, accessed 11/21/2019.
8 From the Sachs and Warner paper cited by Mankiw "Ghana Open since 1985. The black market premium fell from 1,098 percent (average 1981–86) to 3 percent (1990), falling below 20 percent in 1985. In 1990, 0 percent of foreign exchange allocation was controlled, and only two items were subject to non-tariff barriers. The World Bank rates it as a 4 on the export marketing board in 1990, but the discussion in TIDE, p. 191, has no mention of this as a constraint on openness. Hence we rate Ghana as open from 1985", www.brookings.edu/wp-content/uploads/1995/01/1995a_bpea_ sachs_warner_aslund_fischer.pdf, accessed 11/23/2019.
9 www.echosdughana.com/2019/07/09/in-ghana-corruption-disrupts-the-economic-growth/, accessed 11/23/2019.
0 Missing Food: The Case of Postharvest Grain Losses in Sub-Saharan Africa, The World Bank Report #60371-AFR, April 2011, https://siteresources.world bank.org/INTARD/Resources/MissingFoods10_web.pdf, accessed 10/3/2019.

11 www.bog.gov.gh/economic-data/interest-rates/, accessed 10/2/2019.
12 www.focus-economics.com/countries/ghana/news/inflation/inflation-recedes-in-june, accessed 10/2/2019.

Bibliography

Adu, G. (2013). "Determinants of Economic Growth in Ghana: Parametric and Nonparametric Investigations", *The Journal of Developing Areas*, Vol. 47, No. 2, pp. 277–301. doi:10.1353/jda.2013.0027.

Alhassan, H., S.A. Donkoh and Y. Asante (2012). "The Determinants of Long-Term Economic Growth in Ghana from 1960–2007", *Journal of Research in Economics and International Finance*, Vol. 1, No. 5, pp. 141–149.

Ahmad, Eatzaz, Muhammad Aman Ullah and Muhammad Irfanullah Arfeen (2012). "Does Corruption Affect Economic Growth?", *Latin American Journal of Economics*, Vol. 49, No. 2, Santiago versión, ISSN 0719–0433 (Online), http://dx.doi.org/1O.7764/LAJE.49.2.277 Accessed 11/23/2019.

Anaman, K.A. (2006). "What Factors Have Influenced Economic Growth in Ghana?", *The Institute of Economic Affairs (IEA)*, Ghana Policy Analysis 2, Accra.

Antwi, S., E.F. Mills and X. Zhao (2013). "Impact of Macroeconomic Factors on Economic Growth in Ghana: A Co-Integration Analysis", *International Journal of Academic Research in Accounting, Finance, and Management Sciences*, Vol. 3, No. 1, pp. 35–45.

Darko, Christian Kwasi (2015). "Determinants of Economic Growth in Ghana", *EconStor Preprints 123098*, ZBW-Leibniz Information Centre for Economics.

De Soto, Hernando (2000). *The Mystery of Capital: Why Capitalism Triumphs in the West and Fails Everywhere Else*, New York, NY, Basic Books.

Havi, Emmanuel K. Dodzi, Patrick Enu, F. Osei-Gyimah, Prudence Attah-Obeng and C.D.K. Opoku (2013). "Macroeconomic Determinants of Economic Growth in Ghana: Cointegration Approach", *European Scientific Journal*, Vol. 9, No. 19, July, ISSN 1857-7881, pp. 156–175.

Herrera, S. and D. Aykut (2014). "Long-Run Growth in Ghana: Determinants and Prospects", *Policy Research Working Paper; No. 7115*. World Bank Group, Washington, DC. © World Bank, https://openknowledge.worldbank.org/handle/10986/20650 License: CC BY 3.0 IGO, accessed 2/19/2019.

Ho, S.-Y. and B. N. Iyke (2018). "The Determinants of Economic Growth in Ghana: New Empirical Evidence", *Global Business Review*, https://doi.org/10.1177/0972150918779282

King, Elizabeth M., Paul Glewwe and Wim Alberts (1992). "Human Resource and Economic Development Economic Growth: Ghana in the Next Two Decades", *Education and Employment Division, Population and Human Resources Department*, the World Bank, June 30.

Leite, S., A. Pellechio, L. Zanforlin, G. Begashaw, S. Fabrizio, J. Harnack (2000). "Ghana: Economic Development in a Democratic Environment", *International Monetary Fund*, Occasional Paper No. 199. Washington, DC.

Lewis, W.A. (1954). "Economic Development with Unlimited Supply of Labour", *Manchester School of Economic and Social Studies*, Vol. 22, No. 2, pp. 139–191.

Mankiw, Gregory N. (2019). *Macroeconomics* (10th ed.), New York, NY, Worth Publishers.

Ofori, Daniel, Shadrach Ato-Mensah and Jinseng Zhu (2015). "Corruption, Foreign Direct Investment and Growth in Ghana: An Empirical Analysis", *European Journal of Business and Management*, Vol. 7, No. 23, ISSN 2222-1905 (Paper) ISSN 2222-2839 (Online), www.iiste.org Accessed 11/23/2019.

Quraishy, B.B. (1971). "Land Tenure and Economic Development in Ghana", *Présence Africaine*, Nouvelle Série, No. 77 (1er TRIMESTRE 1971), pp. 24–35, Présence Africaine Editions, (Online), www.jstor.org/stable/24349581 Accessed 11/28/2011.

Raggl, A. (2014). "Long-Run Growth in Ghana: Determinants and Prospects", *World Bank Policy Research Working Paper*, No. 6750.

Sachs, Jeffrey D. and Andrew Warner (1995). "Economic Reforms and the Process of Global Integration", Brookings Papers on Economic Activity.

5 Determinants of economic growth in Malaysia

Survey of the literature

Introduction

Review of growth and development in Malaysia

Between 1958 and 1970, Malaysia's real GDP grew at an annual rate average of 5.98% and the real per capita GDP at 3%. In the same period, Ghana's real GDP grew at 4.23% and the real per capita GDP at 1.35%. While these differences are significant, they are nothing compared to what happened between 1971 and 1983. Between those two points in time, the Malaysia real GDP grew at 8.85% and its real per capita GDP at 6.24%; Ghana's real GDP grew a paltry 1.35% and its per capita GDP shrank by −2.94%. By the end of 1983, the real GDP per capita of Malaysia was $7,999.77 – 3.7 times larger than Ghana's $2,074.41. In this chapter we review the literature to identify the factors that contributed to the rapid growth in the Malaysian economy.

Malaysia's growth has been described in terms that border on the miraculous.[1] Like Ghana, it was primarily a primary commodity exporter. It strategically exported its way to growth by mobilizing domestic resources – labor and savings – and creating an environment that was conducive for foreign investors and thereby transformed the structure of its economy from agriculture and mineral extraction to manufacturing and on to high technology. Today Malaysia is a hub for the manufacturing of products for both home and exports. Malaysia's growth path has been steady and relatively smooth. Through a series of five-year development plans, the government directed the economy without being obstructive of the free market it inherited from colonization. Institutions such as the Federal Land Development Authority (FELDA), the Malaysia Industry Development Authority (MIDA), the Malaysia Economic Development Council (MEDC), and the Malaysia Digital Economy (MDEC), which the government established, served as spurs for the economy and not a total replacement for the private sector. Through good and pragmatic policies, a country that was given not much chance of succeeding after independence has managed to build a successful economy that is on the brink on being a developed economy.

Natural resources

Malaysia has an area of about 127,724 square miles (330,803.64 square kilometers), about 1.4 times that of Ghana. Like Ghana, it is a tropical country and well-endowed with natural resources: fertile land for agriculture, minerals, and extensive forests. Malaysia has crude oil deposits of natural gas and liquefied natural gas. These products have enabled Malaysia to earn substantial revenues from exports and to be self-sufficient in energy. Countries like Nigeria discovered oil and suffered what is referred to as the resource curse or the paradox of plenty. In accordance with its deliberate policy of developing slowly, Malaysia did not abandon its agriculture. It continued to mobilize labor to produce agricultural products like rubber, palm oil, cocoa, pineapples and coconuts for domestic consumption and exports.

Macroeconomic environment

Sound macroeconomic policies, social and political stability are sine qua non for economic development. Malaysia appears to have done all of that during the period when the economy was experiencing the most rapid growth. The greatest fear after independence was that the sporadic ethnic violence and communist insurgencies could derail prosperity. Well aware of that, the government in its policies emphasized inclusive growth in the New Economic Policy of the 1970s after the 1969 conflicts. FELDA allocated land to poor people who were willing and able to work in the many settlements it established across the country. This not only generated employment and calmed the waters, but it also led to large tracts of land being cultivated with oil palm trees. Malaysia, unlike Ghana, did not appear to have undertaken major deficit financing. Inflation was low and the exchange rate exhibited little volatility.[2] Between 1957 and 2017 the Malaysian ringgit (RM) on the average exchanged at 3.01 to the US dollar with a standard deviation of 0.54. Even at the height of the Asian currency crisis in the 1990s, the worst it got was 3.92 RM to the dollar in 1997 and was thereafter pegged at 3.80 RM to the dollar. The ability to manage the crisis by buying the RM or selling the dollar, and finally pegging it at 3.80 RM and holding it there gave confidence to foreign investors. Lending rates have been low, averaging 4.56% in the last 40 years, compared to Ghana's of 18.58% (2004 to 2016).[3]

Survey of the literature

The role of exports: before independence and up to the 1960s

The idea that a country can grow through exports seems to be a benign proposition. There is, however, a lively debate about it. Bahman-Oskoee and Alse (1993) provide a review of the state of the literature on the relationship between exports and economic growth. Their study cites other studies that show dual causality in growth and exports for Brazil, Hong Kong, Israel, Korea, and Taiwan, a one-way causality for Mexico (exports to growth), and no causality at all for Argentina. On the other hand, some studies they cite show statistically significant evidence supporting export-led growth (ELG) in 4 out of 37 countries. Yet other studies are not conclusive. The study concludes that there is a long-run positive relationship between real exports and real output. If that is the case, then export-led promotion could be a good strategy to pursue. This is not to say that a closed economy grows faster than an open economy; the latter does and the evidence is clear and does not require discussion. The issue is whether a country can use exports as a strategy to grow out of low-income status. On that, the evidence is mixed.

The importance of exports in the development of Malaysia has been studied by several economists including Doraisami (1996), who tested the hypothesis that exports promoted growth in Malaysia. There are several studies that suggest that open economies grow faster than closed economies because of the benefits derived from interacting with the rest of the world; exposure to new technology and the inflow of capital, and bigger markets for their products. Using a cointegrated error correction model with data from 1963 to 1993, Doraisami concludes that the relationship between exports and economic growth in Malaysia is bidirectional, not unidirectional. This result is not surprising. A small economy benefits from the larger world market to which it exports. The bigger world market enables smaller countries to take advantage of increasing returns to scale and reduce their cost of production.

Between 1920 and 1968, the Malaysian economy depended largely on tin and rubber. In a well-researched paper by Thoburn (1973), he shows how tin and rubber laid the foundation for the rapid growth of the Malaysian economy through the employment of a large number of people and the export revenue derived from them. He argues that these industries (tin and rubber) rather than being enclaves, had reverberations on the economy that enabled Malaysia to pursue its policy of export-oriented development. He points out that large-scale generation of electricity in Malaysia in 1928 was in part the result of the demand for power by tin mining. In turn, the provision of power made it possible for other manufacturing to develop. Thoburn further argues that it is possible that the local production of diesel oil and petroleum products may also have been due to the demand for these products by the tin industry. What this means is that in extracting smelting and exporting tin, important linkages were developed in the economy that helped in growth. Another linkage resulting from the mining of tin was the production of coal and the development of the railway. A substantial portion of the revenue needed for the construction of the railway came from the export of tin. The fact that virtually all the tin produced in Malaysia was smelted locally meant that more valued was added to the commodity and more jobs were created. Similarly, in the production of rubber, more valued was added to the product by manufacturing rubber shoes, tires, and foam rubber. As important as the revenue derived from the export of tin and rubber were, the industries also helped to develop the skills of the local labor force, increasing their earnings and making them employable in other industries requiring technical skills. One could therefore say that to some extent, tin and rubber laid the foundation for Malaysia to become an export-oriented manufacturing hub and grow rapidly.

The 1970s

It was mentioned earlier that Malaysia has always faced tensions because of the multiethnic nature of the society. Perhaps because of it, Malaysia from the very beginning sought to adopt development plans that were inclusive instead of waiting for growth to trickle down. The New Economic Policy (NEP), which began in 1970, was the beginning of such deliberate redistribution of the dividend from growth. In a study by Snodgrass (1995) covering the period 1970–1990, he muses about what would have happened to Malaysia if the NEP had not been initiated and how the country was able to grow while redistributing the growth dividend. Among his observations are that Malaysia's performance was due to the adoption of good policies, good luck, and pragmatism. Unlike Ghana, for example, where inflation sometimes ran wild, Malaysia maintained good monetary, fiscal, and exchange rate policies, keeping inflation low and the exchange rate stable. Good policies can be duplicated, and as has been said elsewhere, good "luck is a matter of preparation meeting opportunity".[4] Perhaps it is in the pragmatic nature of the country that the good performance of the economy derives. In interviews with officials at EPU,[5] the authors were frequently reminded that the various five-year development plans were not static; they were dynamic and were constantly being fine-tuned as needed. Snodgrass gives a good example of Malaysia's pragmatism: In the 1980s, when economic growth slowed down, of the many policy options the government could have pursued, it chose to liberalize the economy – in essence sacrificing redistribution in favor of growth. This change in policy risked alienating the majority of the population for whom the New Economic Policy had given a lifeline. The official justification was that without growth, there will be nothing to redistribute. Snodgrass cites as evidence of pragmatism the tolerant nature of the majority Malays and the Chinese and the United Malays National Organization's willingness to share power with the minority groups, the Chinese and the Indians.

Baharumshah and Almasaied (2009) studied the impact of foreign direct investment (FDI) on growth in Malaysia between 1974 and 2004. During the period under study, average annual net FDI inflows, as a percentage of GDP, was 3.89% compared to Ghana's 1.04%.[6] The results of the study indicate that in the long run, exports, domestic investment, financial deepening, human capital, and FDI all had positive effect on per capita GDP growth. Financial deepening refers to the ease with which different socio-economic groups can access financial services and products and the resulting efficiency in financial intermediation. Some economists argue that poor financial institutions are one of the causes of underdevelopment. By modernizing the financial system therefore, countries remove an obstacle to growth. The study also concludes that domestic investment had the greatest impact on growth, not FDI. In the short run, however, it is FID, higher-level of financial intermediation, higher domestic investment, high exports and human capital that influenced growth. The authors suggest that human capital and financial markets are both important factors for the short term and long term because of their interaction with FDI. In the estimated long-run equations, the interaction of FDI with human capital and financial intermediation were both positive and significant at the 5% level. The positive results from FDI come from its interaction with human capital and financial development, and the positive spillover effects that result. The authors suggest that FDI is probably the main conduit through which advanced technology is transferred into Malaysia and that the absorption of new technology is facilitated by the development of education and the financial system. The importance of human capital in economic development cannot be overstated. Long term growth depends on increasing productivity, that is, getting more output from the same amount of inputs. Increased productivity often comes with the adoption of new improved technology. The ease with which people adopt the new technology in turn depends on many complementary factors including education. The finding that the interaction of FDI and education is a significant factor in Malaysia's economic growth is a confirmation of a fact which human capital advocates stress. Quite often, FDI is the path through which new technology is diffused. Early adopters are those who have appropriate education.

In a study of the determinants of total factor productivity growth in Malaysia between 1971 and 2004, Jajri (2007) concludes that for a great part of the period under study, the strong economic performance displayed by the economy was mostly the result of the country putting more people to work (from 30.5% in 1970 to 39.8% in 2000). Technical progress played only a small portion in increasing total factor productivity. Total factor productivity is the result of education and training, which improves worker efficiency, economic restructuring, which deploys workers from less productive sectors of the economy to more productive sectors (activities where their marginal productivities are low to where they are high), capital structuring, demand intensity, and technical progress. In the discussion of the Solow model, it was noted that in developed economies, it was technological progress which accounts for sustained growth in real gross domestic output per capita. What Jajri's study therefore suggests is that Malaysia may have done very well in increasing growth in the short term but that it has some work to do to sustain it in the long run. Given the strong performance the Malaysian economy has shown in the last 60 years, one cannot bet against the country finding ways to boost technical progress.

Salih, Hwok-Aun and Khalid (2013) in looking at the role of inclusive growth in Malaysia between 1970 and 2013, come to the conclusion that the main driver of growth in Malaysia has been international trade. Over the period under study, Malaysia has managed to move from exporting agricultural products to manufacturing products. This was a period during which Malaysia accumulated surpluses in trade and diversified its economy.

The late 1970s to 2000

We saw earlier that the financial system is an important interactive term with FDI in Malaysia (Baharumshah and Almasaied (2009)). In a discussion paper, Taha, Colombage and Maslyuk (2009) inquire about the relationship between Malaysia's financial system and economic growth. Generally, poor countries have poor financial systems, and as a result financial intermediation is weak. The result is that surplus entities have no efficient means to transfer their surpluses to deficit entities who have productive projects to undertake; thus economic growth is slowed. But is this just a case of correlation of causality? If it is a causality, in which direction does it run? Is it the case that good financial systems promote economic growth or economic growth leads to improved financial systems? Taha et al. cite several sources to argue both sides, including Schumpeter (1912), who argued the importance of financial development for economic development on the grounds that finance can select successful enterprises, and McKinnon (1973) and Shaw (1973), who provided the theoretical underpinnings showing how a well-functioning financial system can promote economic growth. On the other hand, others such as Robinson (1952) and Solow (1956) argue that the financial system has a negligible effect on economic growth. These latter two argue that the price of savings (the supply of loanable funds) and investment (demand for loanable funds), the interest rate, is determined by real factors and finance, has little to do with it; the financial side therefore does not affect economic growth. Students of economics will recognize this argument as the classical economics view point. In the Taha et al. study, search for the direction of causation; does improvement in the financial environment lead to faster economic growth or does economic growth lead to improved financial environment or it is bidirectional; financial development leads to growth, and growth leads to financial development. Using the Kuala Lumpur Composite Index (KLCI) as a proxy for financial development and the Index of Industrial Production (IIP) for economic growth, the authors conclude that the causality is both ways. Tests for Granger causality and Vector Error Correction Model shows the stock market causes economic growth and economic growth causes growth. A study by Ofori-Abebrese, Pickson and Diabah (2017), testing the relationship and the causal direction between financial development and economic growth between 1973 and 2013, the authors conclude that there was a positive significant relationship between domestic credit to the private sector and economic growth in the short run and long run. They also find that causality runs from variations in economic growth to domestic deposits. It is quite plausible that financial markets become causative agents at a certain level of economic growth and not before. Nonetheless, improvements in financial markets are essential for long-term economic growth.

Just about every study of Malaysia during the period 1970s to the 2000s comes to the conclusion that the country's ability to capitalize on exports was a significant factor in its economic transformation. In a paper by Kogid et al. (2010) covering 1970 to 2007 the authors focused on the role household consumption expenditure, government expenditure, exports, the exchange rate and foreign direct investment played in the growth of the economy. All the variables were found by Granger to cause economic growth. There obviously is some simultaneity in the model: consumption, government expenditure and exports are all part of the gross domestic product and therefore would cause GDP to increase; increases in GDP cause consumption and government to also increase. From 1970 to 2000, the range of manufactured goods produced in Malaysia expanded significantly. The economy successfully made the transition from dependence on the export of primary products to manufacturing products for home consumption and the foreign market. In a study by Kamaruddin and Masron (2010) using data covering the period 1970 to 2000, they find that growth in the manufacturing sector was driven by both exports and domestic demand. They suggest that the replacement of import-substitution growth strategy to export-orientation growth in the 1970s and 1980s gave a boost to industrial production. More importantly, manufactured goods such as textiles, electrical, and electronics were not based on the natural resources in Malaysia. The manufacturers of these products were obviously taking advantage of the conducive environment (labor, stability, proximity to markets). While both domestic consumption and exports contributed to increasing the value added in the manufacturing sector, technical efficiency's contribution was actually negative. In essence, what this meant, as observed elsewhere, was that more inputs were being brought into use but their productivities were actually detracting from growth. In the long run, this of course would be a problem.

By the 2000s the Malaysian economy was well diversified. The agriculture and light industry sectors were mostly domestic demand driven. Mining and heavy industry sectors, on the other hand, were mostly export driven; the export sector contributed to about 61% of its growth. The study suggests an economy that began as a primary commodity exporter, turned to import substitution, became an exporter of light manufactured goods and now of heavy industrial goods that are just as likely to be used domestically as exported.

Table 5.1 shows the percentage contribution made by the various sectors to industrial growth between 1978 and 2000. Industrial growth has been driven mostly by domestic demand and exports, and mainly in the heavy industrial sector. The changed structure of the economy and its sustainability can be seen from the following observations from Table 5.1:

1   Domestic demand for heavy industrial products (37%) is about the same as export demand (37.5%);
2   Agriculture's contribution is only 2.8% and the service sector contributed 29.3%, second to heavy industries;
3   There is a reduction in dependence on import substitution (final and intermediate goods), and technology actually distracts from growth (it has a negative sign).

Table 5.1 Sources of industrial growth (% contribution to output growth: 1978–2000)

Sector	Domestic	Export	Import Substitution of		Technological. Change	Total
			Final Goods	Intermediate Goods		
Agriculture	2.8	1.4	−0.1	−1.5	−0.8	1.9
Mining	4.2	4.3	−0.1	−1.2	−0.4	6.8
Light Industries	8.2	6.4	−0.2	−2.3	−2.2	9.9
Heavy Industries	37.0	37.5	−0.8	−5.1	−7.6	61.1
Services	29.3	11.1	−0.7	−8.6	−10.8	20.4
Total	81.5	60.6	−1.8	−18.6	−21.7	100.0

Source: Adapted from table 3, Rohana Kamaruddin and Tajul Ariffin Masron (2010).

This is an economy which has almost completed the typical stages economies go through as they move from underdeveloped to developed.

The advice often given to developing countries as they begin the journey to development is to concentrate on providing infrastructure, as this will encourage the private sector, domestic and/or foreign, to want to do business in the country. If that is the case, then one would expect to see that in developing countries with good infrastructure, growth should be faster than those without good infrastructure. At the time of Ghana's independence, the general consensus was that for an underdeveloped country, it had good infrastructure which should help it grow. Over time, most of the infrastructure was allowed to deteriorate, and it is only in recent years that serious efforts are being made to fix it. In a report by the World Bank, in 2017, it was noted that closing the quality and quantity of the infrastructure "gap relative to the best performers in the world could increase the growth of GDP per capita by 2.6% per year".[7] One could infer that that this would be the case in all countries. In an article by Bakar, Mat and Harun (2012), the authors sought to determine the impact infrastructure had on Malaysia's growth between 1970 and 2010. As well, they sought to look at the impact of market size, trade openness and human capital on foreign direct investment. The study concludes that there is a significant positive relationship between infrastructure and FDI. This is as expected. Businesses, whether domestic or foreign, want to locate where there is power, ease of transportation (good road networks, easy access to air and sea ports), and good communication connections internally and with the rest of the world. The size of the market was also found to be positive and significant as was openness to trade. The interesting finding was that human capital showed a significant negative relationship in attracting foreign direct investment. The explanation given by the authors, which sounded reasonable, was that the type of FDI going into Malaysia was looking for labor intensive and cost minimizing in the manufacturing sector, which does not depend on highly educated workers. This is reassuring in the sense that the finding does not dismiss investment in human capital but seeks to make the point that gestation of that type of human capital takes a little longer to produce results.

Hussin, Ros and Noor (2013), on the determinants of growth in Malaysia between 1970 and 2010, looked at trade openness, FDI, government development expenditure and gross fixed capital formation and their impact on GDP. Trade openness, government development expenditure and gross fixed capital formation were found to have significant positive effects on GDP. FDI was found to be negatively related to GDP. In the short run, the authors conclude that trade openness had a negative relationship to GDP. On the surface, this suggest that being a closed economy could enhance growth, which seems at odds with most studies. Further, the importance of FDI in making new technology available and boosting growth suggest that there may have been misspecification or that some interactive terms are missing. In the Baharumshah and Almasaied (2009) study cited earlier, there was the suggestion that FDI works interactively through human capital and financial markets. Perhaps the absence of the interactive terms in the model specification may account for why FDI and openness show negative impacts on GDP. In a later study by Aziz and Azmi (2017), covering the period 1982 to 2013, they concluded that FDI is the only significant factor that positively affected GDP. Female labor force participation also showed a positive impact but it was not significant while inflation was negative but also insignificant. The Aziz and Azmi study is in sharp contrast with the Hussin, Ros and Noor (2013) which found FDI to be negatively related to GDP.

In a more recent article on the causes of growth in Malaysia, Hashim and Masih (2014) looked at the role of both exports and imports as well as the exchange rate in the growth and other variables in the growth of the Malaysian economy between 2005 and 2014. They sought to tease out whether Malaysia's growth was export led, (ELG), import led (ILG), or growth led (GLG). They conclude that Malaysia's growth was significantly affected by both exports and imports, in other words it was both export led and import led. Exports are, however exogenous, but imports are endogenously determined. Essentially, policies on promoting exports and the increase in exports induces changes in imports. They also find that there is a bidirectional causal relationship between GDP growth and exports and between imports and GDP growth. Lastly, there is a bidirectional long-run association between exports and imports

The idea of export-led growth (ELG) in the literature means that a country could focus on producing and exporting the goods for which it has comparative advantage and make the exports a leading sector in growth. Exports generate income for households, proceeds for business investment and revenue for governments expenditure. In recent times, all the countries that have successfully developed have done so using this strategy. The countries include Singapore, China and South Korea. To a large extent Malaysia has done so, beginning with the colonial exports of tin and rubber and then into light manufactured goods and now into heavy industrialized goods. In all cases there was a deliberate effort on the part of policy makers to promote exports. The idea also harks back to the mercantilist philosophy of exporting as much as possible while importing as little as possible to ensure that specie (mostly gold and silver then) flows in but not out. Export promotion as a strategy for economic growth will be effective if import restrictions are maintained. The problem is that import restrictions can sometimes promote retaliations from trading partners. The US, for example, has had frequent conflicts with trading partners on account of this, in the 1980s with Japan and in recent times with China, accusing both of placing barriers to trade which favored their exports but restricted their imports. For the foregoing reasons, even countries that use an export-led growth strategy are still dependent on imports. Moroke, Ntebogang Dinah and Molebogeng Manoto (2015) found this to be true for South Africa.

Summary and conclusions

The literature review indicates that, for the most part, Malaysia's growth has been propelled by mobilizing its resources fully. As indicated in Jajri (2007), during the 1970 to 2007 period, when Malaysia rapidly transformed its economy, the expansion was mostly the result of putting more people to work. He further suggests that technical progress played only a small portion in increasing total factor productivity. This would suggest that the correct policies, implemented correctly could go a long way towards improving growth. The New Economic Policy (NEP), which began in 1970 and had as one of its goals *inclusive growth*, did a lot to reduce poverty and move the economy towards increased production. The creation of settlements under the FELDA plan ensured that those willing and able to work would be supported to become employed. As observed earlier, Snodgrass (1995), the NEP enabled Malaysia to not only grow but to also redistribute the dividend from growth to reduce poverty and bring into the mainstream some previously marginalized people. Another equally important way the economy was able to grow was through the mobilization of domestic savings and here again the formation of Permodalan Nasional Berhad (PNB) in 1978 was instrumental. By making it easy and attractive to save, many more people did so, providing the means to buy into new businesses and into old ones as well.

FDI appears to be significant in all the studies cited. To attract FDI, the environment must be conducive and it was in Malaysia. Inflation was low, the exchange rate was stable, and the economy was for the most part open. Even during the Asian currency crisis which began in July 1997, Malaysia was able to ride the storm by using a combination of policies: selling dollars to prevent the currency from depreciating too quickly, pursuing a tight monetary and contractionary fiscal policies and finally, pegging the Malaysian ringgit at 3.80 to US$1 after it appeared that none of the other policies would stem the tide. The pegging stayed in place until 2004. The result was that even though the economy contracted by 4.6% between 1997 and 1998, between 1998 and 1999 it rebounded and grew at 6.87% and 7.61% between 1999 to 2000. The willingness to do what was necessary to ensure that the economy is stable is what has been described by Snodgrass (1995) as pragmatism. The favorable macroeconomic climate ensured that businesses could plan over a long horizon and this encouraged foreign direct investment.

In the study by Baharumshah and Almasaied (2009), they conclude that the positive results from FDI come from interaction with human capital and financial development, and that this is probably the main conduit through which advanced technology is transferred into Malaysia. Malaysia's 2018 Human Development Index (HCI)[8] of 0.65 suggests that investments in human capital have been made to improve the education and health of its labor force.

A good infrastructure is essential for economic growth. Intuitively, one would expect that countries with better infrastructure would attract FDI. That, according to the literature, is the case for Malaysia. With the export surpluses, the government concentrated on building good infrastructure needed for businesses to operate efficiently. It does not hurt that both Peninsular and Eastern Malaysia are surrounded by water and thus make transportation easier. Its location near China, Japan and the Asian Tigers (Hong Kong, Singapore, South Korea and Taiwan) no doubt made an impact. Investment in human capital has also enable Malaysia to grow.

One of the inescapable conclusions from the literature is the role exports played in Malaysia's growth. Malaysia has benefited from the exports of tin and rubber as well as oil palm products. At a time when the demand for oil for industrial purposes was growing in the 1920s Malaysia took advantage. The palm oil was then processed and exported in large quantities. In the 1970s, rubber plantations enabled it to make and export rubber products for domestic and industrial uses. It emulated its neighbors by using exports as the spur to growth.

Notes

1 Stiglitz, Joseph, www.theguardian.com/commentisfree/2007/sep/13/themalaysian miracle, accessed 11/25/2019.
2 PWT9.1.
3 Source: International Financial Statistics (IFS).
4 This quote has been attributed to talk show host Oprah Winfrey. Luck is a matter of preparation meeting opportunity.
5 Summer 2018, in Kuala Lumpur.
6 World Development Indicators, https://data.worldbank.org/indicator/bx.klt.dinv. wd.gd.zs, accessed 4/24/2019.
7 *Why We Need to Close the Infrastructure Gap in Sub-Saharan Africa*, April 2017, www.worldbank.org/en/region/afr/publication/why-we-need-to-close-the-infrastructure-gap-in-sub-saharan-africa World Bank Publication, accessed 10/23/2019.
8 Human Capital Index, The World Bank, accessed 10/30/2019.

Bibliography

Aziz, R. and A. Azmi (2017). "Factor Affecting Gross Domestic Product (GDP) Growth in Malaysia", *International Journal of Real Estate Studies*, Vol. 11, No. 4.

Baharumshah, A.Z. and S.W. Almasaied (2009). "Foreign Direct Investment and Economic Growth in Malaysia: Interactions with Human Capital and Financial Deepening", *Emerging Markets Finance and Trade*, Vol. 45, No. 1, pp. 90–102. doi:10.2753/ree1540-496x450106.

Bahman-Oskoee, Mohsen and Janardhanan Alse (1993). "Export Growth and Economic Growth: An Application of Cointegration and Error-Correction Modeling", *The Journal of Developing Areas*, Vol. 27, No. 4, pp. 535–542.

Bakar, N.A., S.C. Mat and M. Harun (2012). "The Impact of Infrastructure on Foreign Direct Investment: The Case of Malaysia", *Procedia-Social and Behavioral Sciences*, Vol. 65, pp. 205–211.

"Changing Drivers of Economic Growth in Malaysia", (2012). *Economic Developments in 2012*, Annual Report, pp. 34–39.

Doraisami, A. (1996). "Export Growth and Economic Growth: A Reexamination of Some Time-Series Evidence of the Malaysian Experience", *The Journal of Developing Areas*, pp. 223–230.

Hashim, K. and M. Masih (2014). "What Causes Economic Growth in Malaysia: Exports or Imports?", *Munich Personal RePEc Archive (MPRA)*.

Hussin, F., N.M. Ros and M.S.Z. Noor (2013). "Determinants of Economic Growth in Malaysia 1970–2010", *Asian Journal of Empirical Research*, Vol. 3, No. 9, pp. 1165–1176.

Jajri, I. (2007). "Determinants of Total Factor Productivity Growth in Malaysia", *Journal of Economic Cooperation*, Vol. 28, No. 3, pp. 41–58.

Kamaruddin, R. and T.A. Masron (2010). "Sources of Growth in the Manufacturing Sector in Malaysia: Evidence from Ardl and Structural Decomposition Analysis", *Asian Academy of Management Journal*, Vol. 15, No. 1, pp. 99–116.

Kogid, M., D. Mulok, L.F.Y. Beatrice and K. Mansur (2010). "Determinant Factors of Economic Growth in Malaysia: Multivariate Cointegration and Causality Analysis", *European Journal of Economics, Finance and Administrative Sciences*, Vol. 24, pp. 123–133.

McKinnon, R.I. (1973). *Money and Capital in Economic Development*, Washington, DC, The Brookings Institution.

Moroke, Ntebogang Dinah and Molebogeng Manoto (2015). "How Applicable Is Export-Led Growth and Import-Led Growth Hypotheses to South African Economy the VECM and Causality Approach", *Journal of Governance and Regulation*, Vol. 4, No. 2.

New Straits Times (2017). "Celebrating 100 Years of Malaysian Palm Oil (Part 1)", www.nst.com.my/news/nation/2017/05/240770/celebrating-100-years-malaysian-palm-oil-part-1, accessed 12/3/2018.

Ofori-Abebrese, G., R. Pickson and B. Diabah (2017). "Financial Development and Economic Growth: Additional Evidence from Ghana", *Modern Economy*, Vol. 8, pp. 282–297. doi:10.4236/me.2017.82020, www.scirp.org/(S(lz5mqp453edsnp55rrgjct55))/journal/paperinformation.aspx?paperid=74328, accessed 10/18/2019.

Robinson, J. (1952). *The Rate of Interest and Other Essays*. London, MacMillan & Co Ltd, see also Arestis, P. and Malcolm Sawyer (2005). "Financial Liberalization and the Finance-Growth Nexus: What Have We Learned", in *Financial Liberalization: Beyond Orthodox Concerns*, edited by P. Arestis and Malcolm Sawyer, London, Palgrave/Macmillan.

Salih, K., L. Hwok-Aun and M.A. Khalid (2013). "Analytics of Inclusive Growth in Malaysia", *Malaysia Human Development Report 2013: Redesigning an Inclusive Future*, pp. 80–107.

Schumpeter, J.A. (1912). *The Theory of Economic Development*, Cambridge, MA, Harvard University Press.

Shaw, E. (1973). *Financial Deepening in Economic Development*, Oxford, Oxford University Press.

Snodgrass, D.R. (1995). "Successful Economic Development in a Multi-Ethnic Society: The Malaysian Case", *Harvard Institute for International Development*, Harvard University.

Solow, R.M. (1956). "A Contribution to the Theory of Economic Growth", *The Quarterly Journal of Economics*, Vol. 70, No. 91, pp. 65–94.

Stiglitz, J. (2007). "Fifty Years of Independence: Reflections on Malaysia's Past and Future", Speech delivered for the Khazanah Global Lectures Series, Kuala Lumpur, Malaysia.

Taha, R., S.R. Colombage and S. Maslyuk (2009). "Financial Development and Economic Growth in Malaysia: Cointegration and Co-Feature Analysis", Monash University, Department of Economics.

Thoburn, J.T. (1973). "Exports and Economic Growth in West Malaysia", *Oxford Economic Papers*, Vol. 25, No. 1, pp. 88–111.

6 Summary, recommendations, and conclusions

Introduction

The overarching goal of the book is to understand the disparity in growth performance between Malaysia and Ghana in the roughly 60-year period after both nations attained independence from the British in 1957. In and of itself, this is an interesting academic exercise. More importantly, however, it could provide some useful insights for policy makers in the lessons learned. As has been observed, Malaysia is an upper-middle-income country with a real per capita GDP of close to $25,000 – about five times that of Ghana's $5,200 as of 2017.[1] About the time of independence, Ghana's per capita GDP of US$2,640.56 was slightly higher than that of Malaysia's, which was about US$2,521.89, primarily because Malaysia had a bigger population (7.68 million) versus Ghana (6.07 million). By 1964, Malaysia's real GDP per capita had overtaken that of Ghana and thereafter the gap between the two countries only got wider. Throughout the 1970s, when Ghana was struggling to lift off, Malaysia had already taken off and its real GDP per capita was growing at about 6.79% a year. At that rate, the Malaysian economy was doubling in size about every ten years. During the same period, the Ghanaian economy shrank by an average of about 1% annually, declining by as much as 14.51% in 1975 and 5.5% in 1976. There is no doubt that some of the factors that caused this difference in economic performance may have been outside the control of policy makers. There may have been some bad luck (no rains and poor harvest) or good luck (the price of cocoa or rubber taking a sudden jump). Over the stretch of 60 or more years, however, it is more than likely that it is neither good luck nor bad luck that dictated how the two economies have fared; rather, it is the result of good or bad economic policies.

The specific objectives of the book are as follows:

1 To identify the determinants of growth in both countries;
2 To identify and examine the specific policies pursued by Ghana and Malaysia immediately after independence and their short-term and long-term impacts on the economy;

3   To determine the extent to which the successful Malaysian policies could be duplicated in Ghana, or indeed elsewhere in Africa.

Policies pursued

From the onset, Malaysia recognized the importance of continuity. Perhaps the single most important piece of action taken or not taken was the decision to retain the colonial civil servants and let them run the affairs of state until the Malaysians themselves were ready to take over. This is where politics and nationalist aspirations sometimes clash. Having fought so hard to attain independence, it is difficult then to allow the country to be run by the colonial masters. In the case of Ghana, it was argued that the Ghanaians were capable of running their own affairs and so there was no need to retain the expatriates.[2] The colonial officers were encouraged to depart. Malaysia retained the market economy it had inherited from the British. While it recognized that the colonial system had not treated everybody equally well – the British, the Chinese, and the Indians had fared better than the Malays – Malaysia was not in haste to change the economic structure to make immediate amends; it would do that over time. The desire to maintain the status quo meant continuing to favor the British, the Chinese, and the Indians. The ensuing ethnic conflicts in the late 1960s pressed home the need to hasten the changes. This ushered in the New Economic Policy of the 1970s and with it the deliberate effort to bring the marginalized into the economic mainstream by adopting inclusive growth. Inclusive growth did not seek to redress past inequities by taking from current wealth holders; instead, it sought to redistribute future growth to slowly bring about parity. To some extent, Ghana faced a similar problem. Colonial and post-colonial development had been mostly in the south. While the cocoa industry made many in the south very wealthy, there was no one such crop in the north to make them as rich; this disparity in development between the north and the south still exists.

As stated in an earlier chapter, while Malaysia was pursuing a slow and steady development path, it does appear that Ghana was pursuing a hasty and uneven development path. The decision to indigenize the civil service in Ghana, may have been very gratifying to a newly independent country. The new prime minister recognized the difficulty of mobilizing resources to develop the economy. He knew that some capital had to come from abroad. His dilemma is captured in the following quote:

> the problem is how to obtain capital investment and still keep it under sufficient control to prevent exploitation; and how to preserve integrity and sovereignty without crippling economic or political ties to any country, bloc or system.

> (*Africa Must Unite*, Kwame Nkrumah)

The concern with preserving the freedom the new country has just won will in time lead the country to abandon the free market economic system it had inherited from its colonial past, and turn to socialism as the quickest way to hasten economic development. This happened explicitly in the Seven-Year Development Plan (SYDP) introduced in 1964. The Ghanaian government stated that to speed up the rate of growth of the economy, it was going to embark upon a socialist transformation of the same through the rapid development of the state and cooperative sectors and at the same time get rid of the colonial structure of the economy. A large number of state-owned enterprises were set up or expanded to engage in activities which had up to then been in the exclusive province of the private sector. Such large intrusion into businesses such as agriculture, hospitality, manufacture of consumer goods, hospitality, and so forth meant a substantial portion of government expenditure that could have gone for infrastructure and social development had to be diverted to the industries. Further, with an export base that was and is still largely dependent on one major commodity, cocoa, whose prices fluctuated widely, the country could not accumulate the funds needed for the ambitious plan; some of the funds had to come from elsewhere.[3] The elsewhere included monetizing some of the deficit and borrowing from abroad. The former began the slow process of inflation which accelerated in the 1970s and 1980s. It also led to foreign exchange controls; both currency and imports. Fundamentally, the plan had an internal conflict; a country that had expressly stated that it was using a socialist blueprint for development was at the same time expecting private capital from abroad to help in the development. The conclusion was that it was all right for foreigners to be in the private sector, but not Ghanaians. The change in the direction of the economy from private to socialist and the consequent inefficiencies in the state enterprises, stayed with the country long after Ghana had abandoned the socialist model of economic growth.

Both Ghana and Malaysia pursued a policy of import substitution industrialization. Import substitution requires a steady and adequate supply of raw materials and a market size big enough for the industries to be able to produce at the minimum efficient scale of operation. The size of the market is a function of not only the population but also of income. Both countries had relatively small populations and low income. Malaysia overcame the market limitation by coupling import substitution with an aggressive export orientation approach. The country processed the primary products which it produced, rubber and palm oil, and was thus able to add more value to its exports leverage the skills acquired into other manufacturing.

Ghana's ISI was based on the availability of locally produced agricultural inputs. The problem was that because of low productivity in the agriculture sector, the supply of inputs was not dependable and the enterprises operated at excess capacity. The meat factory, the tomato processing factory, the rice and oil mills all suffered from an unreliable supply chain. In the end, the state enterprises became sinkholes and yet they could not be readily abandoned. Some of them lingered on into the 2000s (Ghana Airways, State Transport Corporation), still racking up debts.

After several years of Ghana seeking to diversify its export basket, as late as between 2015 to 2017, ten commodities accounted for 88% of the total value of exports. These comprised, with the exception of petroleum oils and oils obtained from bituminous minerals, gold, cocoa and a miniscule of manufactured products: tableware, kitchenware, other household articles and toilet articles. By contrast, the top ten commodities exported by Malaysia accounted for only about 46% of the value derived from exports. Although Malaysian exports still include palm oil and its fractions and petroleum oils, the basket of exports is a diversified bundle made up of electronic integrated circuits, diodes, and transistors as well as parts and accessories for machines.[4] Most of these products are meant for the domestic as well as the international market.

If an economy has a diversified basket of exports, the revenues derived from the total basket can withstand fluctuations in international prices better for the simple reason that not all prices will move down at the same time. A decrease in the price of cocoa, for example, can be offset by an increase in the price of some other commodities in the basket and thus reduce the variation in export revenues. This was the reason Governor Guggisberg as far back as the 1920s, talked about the "four large baskets" comprising groundnuts, shea butter, oil palm, and cocoa and the seven little baskets, comprising rice, copra, sisal, corn, sugar, coffee, and tobacco. Tobacco may have gone out of favor, but the other commodities could have become the basses for agribusiness.

The inability of Ghana to diversify its exports and its dependence on a few primary commodities was and still remains an obstacle. Fluctuations in the price of cocoa, still a major export item, tends to wreak havoc with the entire government budget and the orderly development of infrastructure.

Determinants of growth in Ghana and Malaysia

Stability

A factor that is very significant for economic growth which was present in Malaysia, but decidedly absent in Ghana during the critical period of the 1970s and 1980s, was political stability. It is true that Malaysia experienced some disturbances in the form of ethnic conflicts. Compared to Ghana, however, Malaysia has been relatively stable since independence. One party has always been in power or has been dominant in the ruling coalition. There is no doubt that this stability has been helpful in Malaysia's growth. Political stability may not be the norm in human history, but as Hussain (2014) argues, it is inextricably linked to economic development. Frequent changes in the government can create a lack of confidence for businesses and discourage foreign direct investment. This does not necessarily mean that political stability will always lead to economic development; its absence, however, is detrimental. Ghana has had several bouts of instability, mostly the result of coups d'état or fear of them. Including the first civilian government formed after independence, there has been a total of 12 different administrations in Ghana. In and of itself, this is not anomalous, since it means that on the average, there is a new administration about every five years. What is disruptive is the means by which the administrations are changed. In the 62 years since independence, 38 of those years had military governments. Unfortunately, in Ghana the military did not always have the best plans or personnel to rule the country. Dartey-Baah (2015) argues that the military regimes were characterized by chaos, violence and human rights abuses, while the civilian governments were characterized by predictability and stability.

It is not by accident that the period between 1967 and 1986, when military takeovers were taking place, also saw the worst growth performance in Ghana. For Malaysia, the same period produced some of the best growth performances in economic performance. Whenever there is a change in government, even in the best of times, it takes a while for the new administration to reorient itself to the economic realities. When the change is sudden and unplanned, it takes even longer. Studies such as Anaman (2006) and Alhassan et al. (2012) suggest that the frequent changes in government may have slowed Ghana's progress. Indeed, the studies saw conclude that there is a positive significant relationship between political stability in Ghana and economic growth. The data bears this out. The longest period of uninterrupted growth in real GDP has been from 1984 to date and except for 2015, so has the real GDP per capita.

Stability in a country breeds confidence in investors; confidence encourages FDI, which for many developing countries is both a source of loanable funds (savings, equity capital) and the transfer of technology. The data show that between 1975 and 2005, the flow of FDI into Malaysia, as percentage of GDP, was 10.53 times higher than Ghana. There is no data for Ghana prior to 1975 but between 1970 and 1974, Malaysia was averaging FDI inflow of 3.06% of GDP.[5] Baharumshah and Almasaied (2009) and several others show the positive impact of FDI in Malaysia's economic growth. Havi et al. (2013) also show that FDI has a positive impact in Ghana. This means that for both countries, the more FDI they got, the faster their economies grew. Since Ghana got less, one can conclude that its economy grew less.

Exports

For both countries, exports were and are still very important for economic growth. Whether or not the causality is unidirectional (exports to growth) or bidirectional (exports to growth, growth to exports), the evidence shows that for both Malaysia and Ghana, exports played significant roles in their economies; they create employment, bring in income which increases consumption, and more importantly, provide the revenue for infrastructure development and so forth. They also enable the country to import inputs that may be absent in the domestic economy, especially new technology. For both countries, the main exports were initially primary unprocessed or semi-processed goods. Over time, Malaysia's export basket changed significantly; it now comprises more manufactured products and has more diversity. Ghana's export basket still remains mainly primary products. In recent times, its top ten export products account for 88% of all export revenue; Malaysia's account for under 50%. The inability of Ghana to diversify its export basket has meant that it depends on a few commodities whose prices fluctuate quite a lot (gold, cocoa, and in recent times, petroleum). The fluctuations make it difficult for long-term planning which is critical for growth. In the early mid-1960s, the precipitous decline in cocoa prices by about 25%, from 1963/1964 to 1965/1965 (prices fell from US$522 to US$389 per tonne) probably contributed to the general disaffection with the government, and made it easier for Ghanaians to accept the first coup in February 1966.

Macroeconomic and financial environment

The financial environment also appears to have been favorable for development in Malaysia. Mobilizing domestic savings is very important. The ease with which different socio-economic groups can access financial services (saving or borrowing) is an important factor in economic growth. Some economists argue that poor financial institutions are one of the causes of underdevelopment. By modernizing the financial system therefore, countries remove an obstacle to growth. In Malaysia, domestic investment has had a big impact on growth. One study suggests that it is domestic investment and not FDI, that has had the greatest impact on growth. As Table 6.1 shows, in the decades 1960 to 1979, the pace of increase in domestic investment in Malaysia was frenetic; several times more than Ghana.

Table 6.1 shows that Ghana is now catching up. The main point is that the divergence in growth between Malaysia and Ghana can also be attributed to the significance differences in the rate at which their savings grew. The same macroeconomic environment makes it easier for FDI. Several factors impede FDI, including political and social instability, unpredictable macroeconomic

Table 6.1 Percentage changes in domestic savings Ghana and Malaysia

Percentage Change
Gross Domestic Savings

Decade	MYS	GHA	MYS/GHA
1960–1969	121.16	5.10	23.76
1970–1979	33.46	9.67	3.46
1980–1989	7.61	5.48	1.39
1990–1999	11.25	47.38	0.24
2000–2009	8.42	29.07	0.29
2010–2017	4.35	164.14	0.03

Source: https://data.worldbank.org/indicator/NY.GDS.TOTL.CD?locations=MY.

policies, opaque laws and institutions, and so forth. The laws and regulations and the lack of transparency makes it difficult for both domestic and foreign investment. Of the 190 countries ranked by the World Bank on the ease of doing business, Malaysia ranks 15th (moved to 12 in 2019) and Ghana 118th in 2018 (fell to 18 in 2019), out of 190 countries. It is several times easier to do business in Malaysia than Ghana.[6] There is no reason to think that the past was any different. The idea behind the statistic is that "economic activity requires good rules and regulations that are efficient" to users. In Malaysia, there is one stop for foreign business seeking to invest. In recent times Ghana has adopted such an investment friendly climate as well. The problem has always been that even when the rules were in existence in Ghana, the lack of transparency made it difficult to know what and how to do it. As many cynics have commented, this creates the avenues for corruption.

Corruption and institutions

One cannot talk about economic growth in Ghana without mentioning corruption.[7] It may be the case that there is corruption everywhere, but some countries can afford it; some cannot. In the review of the literature, there is no mention of corruption being an impediment to growth in Malaysia.[8] In Ghana, it has definitely been an impediment to growth. Where there is corruption, institutions do not function properly and incentives tend to be misdirected. More importantly, in its many forms, corruption increases the cost of doing business for both domestic and foreign firms.[9] Good institutions are essential for the orderly operation of a society. Acemoglu and Robinson (2012) cite appropriate economic institutions, open pluralistic societies and inclusive political institutions as important for growth. One could also argue that institutions are as good as the people who are running them. As mentioned earlier, of the 190 countries in the world, the World Bank ranks

Ghana as 118 (2019) on the ease of doing business index; Malaysia ranks 12th (2019). Where is there is corruption, doing business is costly. The cost comes not only from the payments that must be made to circumvent bureaucracy, but also from not knowing what to do to get the right thing done. Processing documents for business formation or to get a permit to do anything should in theory be relatively straightforward. In Ghana, it is often the case that there is no place or anybody who can point you to the place to go and find the information.[10] More often than not, the personnel need inducements to get them to do what they are paid to do. For large businesses, these costs may be easily overcome. For small businesses, it may mean not registering the business at all. In Chapter 4 we mentioned that the Ghanaian Center for Democratic Development estimates the cost of corruption to the government at close to US$2 billion over a three-year period.[11] We also cited the study by Ofori et al. (2015), who suggested that corruption reduces the inflow of FDI. Corrupt institutions and officials prevent economic progress. In the review of the literature on Malaysia, not one of them mentioned corruption as an impediment to growth. Again, it is not the case that corruption does not exist in Malaysia; it appears that the government has worked very hard to minimize it. The lack of transparency and accountability have been at the base of corruption. The advent of free press and the internet appear to be making a dent in Ghana.

Can the success be duplicated?

No two paths to economic growth are ever the same. In the case of Ghana and Malaysia, however, it does appear that Ghana could have easily duplicated what Malaysia did. There is nothing in the literature and the theories reviewed to suggest that Ghana could not have achieved the same success. This leads us to the conclusion that the reason Ghana fell behind Malaysia in growth has to do with the economic policies pursued, which in turn were guided by the philosophies that guided the post-independent leaders. Malaysia's decision to continue on the market-oriented, silent state intervention approach where appropriate meant that in the short run, it had to endure the unequal economic stations of the various ethnic groups. The New Economic Policy (NEP), which emphasized inclusive economic development, led to the creation of institutions which enabled Malaysia to mobilize domestic resources (savings and labor) and to attract foreign direct investment to grow very quickly in the 1970s. According to Navaratnam (1997), the earlier plans, put together with help from the World Bank, sought to build infrastructure first. This is advice which Ghana received and pursued parsimoniously. At independence, Ghana had good infrastructure, but in the haste to grow, it began to direct resources into areas which should have been left to the private sector. Malaysia's plans allowed the private sector to make its own plans within the framework of the government's long-term plans.

Keeping inflation low and the exchange rate stable are policy variables which every government can implement or not. Low inflation and a stable exchange rate are important because they create confidence in the economy. High inflation is invariably the result of excess money supply when other sources of government revenue are insufficient to meet government expenditures.[12] Malaysia pursued a policy of a balanced budget and thus avoided deficit financing.

Malaysia's Five-Year Development Plans benefited from stability in government. In all the plans, the Economic Planning Unit (EPU) has been the principal agent through which the plans are formulated, implemented, monitored, evaluated and revised as it is implemented. It has been doing so since its establishment in 1961.[13] Because it reports directly to the prime minister and includes it's composition ensures that it gets all the cooperation from all government agencies. EPU formulates, implements, monitors, and evaluates progress and makes revisions. That one unit is able to do these important functions for such a long period of time means that personnel develop expertise which they can pass on. In Ghana, different regimes came up with different economic planning units, none of which continued with the plans of the previous regime.

When people say that Malaysia was lucky, there may be an element of truth in it. It is well situated in the tropics, has fertile land and rich forest, a long coastline, and is close to countries that demonstrate that one can prosper with hard work. Malaysia had a lot going for it. It also had problems which could have made it difficult to become a cohesive society to develop. The unequal distribution of wealth during colonial times, which saw the indigenous Malays at the bottom, and the Chinese and Indians at the top, just behind the colonial British, and sometimes led to ethnic riots, could have thwarted all hopes of economic prosperity.

In the 1920s, when industrialization was in full bloom in Europe, Malaysia benefited from its exports of rubber and oils to the new industries. Blessed with oil which it began exploiting in earnest in the 1950s, oil never dominated the economy nor did it distort the structure. It is ranked as number 28 in the work in proven oil reserves.[14] More than luck, it is the policy decisions Malaysia pursued that made the difference. Similarly, it is the policy decisions Ghana pursued after independence that made the difference.

One can engage in a what-if exercise and imagine what would have happened to Ghana if:

1   It had not encouraged the British expatriates to leave soon after independence but had been patient enough to develop the local talent to ease them out;

2 It had not been as ambitious and had proceeded as slowly as Malaysia did in its quest for growth;
3 It had focused on developing its infrastructure and encouraged the private sector to develop;
4 It had spent the same amount of resources developing and increasing productivity in the other three products in the "four big baskets" and the "seven little baskets" before setting up the factories to use the inputs from some of them;
5 It had not turned to socialism as the best way to develop its economy but had, instead continued with the free market policies it inherited from the British.

All these questions are of course hypothetical. Nonetheless, it does not take much of a stretch to see what could have happened. In terms of natural resources, Ghana was not much different from Malaysia: a tropical climate and fertile land that could allow it to grow several varieties of crops, a forest filled with timber and minerals that were in demand, a relatively homogeneous group of people, and at independence, a standard of living that was higher than Malaysia's.

There is no doubt that the change in orientation from a market economy to a socialist one delayed progress. There is also no doubt that the instabilities or fear of them, that occurred in the country in the 1960s through the 1980s and perhaps did not end until the beginning 2000s held the country back.

Circumstances are never the same. A country can pursue good policies to take advantage of propitious events when they occur, but it cannot pursue bad polices to take advantage of propitious events when they occur. Perhaps it may be more difficult for Ghana to grow using the same good policies as Malaysia did in the 1970s; perhaps not. The rapid progress Ghana has made in the past ten years or less suggests that stability and good policies can still promote growth. What Malaysia has done, Ghana can do. It takes sound policies, time, and patience.

Notes

1 www.rug.nl/ggdc/productivity/pwt/, accessed 7/2/2019.
2 Actually Ghana continued to depend on expatriate expertise for a long time, especially in education and in the delivery of health care. In education the British Council continued to send teachers to Ghana through the late 1960s. Ghana was also the first country to receive US Peace Corps volunteers.
3 Between 1960 and 2015, the average price per tonne of cocoa has been US$1,654 with a standard deviation of US$867. Source: International Cocoa Organization, *QBCS*, Vol. XLII No 1 Cocoa Year 2015/2016.

4 https://comtrade.un.org/pb/downloads/2018/Vol12018.pdf, pp. 152, 218, accessed 4/11/2019.
5 International Monetary Fund, Balance of Payments database, supplemented by data from the United Nations Conference on Trade and Development and official national sources.
6 World Bank, Doing Business project (doingbusiness.org). Ease of doing business index (1 = most business-friendly regulations).
7 Hutchful, Eboe, "From Revolution to Monetarism: The Economics and Politics of the Adjustment Programme in Ghana", in *Structural Adjustment in Africa*, Edited by Bonnie K. Campbell and John Loxley. London, Macmillan Press, 1989, pp. 92–131.
8 In Malaysia, the case of the 1MBD scandal involving some one billion dollars has dominated the news.
9 www.ghanaweb.com/GhanaHomePage/features/10-Ways-In-Which-Corruption-Hampers-Economic-Development-207109, accessed 11/5/2019.
10 Information on state enterprises are often not made public. One of the authors (Andoh) spent several months trying to locate any copy of the Annual Audited Report of Ghana Airways and was unsuccessful in the usual places one would have expected to find such a document, including the library at the Parliament House.
11 www.echosdughana.com/2019/07/09/in-ghana-corruption-disrupts-the-economic-growth/, accessed 11/23/2019.
12 In Ghana, a story is told of one of the military men who had taken over the government been informed that there was no money in the government's coffers. He asked to be taken to the Central Bank's vaults to verify this. This may not be taken literally, but it points to the lack of understanding of how the economy works by people who wanted to fix what was wrong with it.
13 https://knoema.com/atlas/sources/EPU, accessed 11/30/2019.
14 https://knoema.com/atlas/topics/Energy/Oil/Crude-oil-reserves?baseRegion= MY, accessed 11/30/2019.

Bibliography

Acemoglu, Daron and James A. Robinson (2012). *Why Nations Fail: The Origins of Power, Prosperity and Poverty* (1st ed.). New York, Crown, p. 529.

Alhassan, H., S.A. Donkoh and Y. Asante (2012). "The Determinants of Long-Term Economic Growth in Ghana from 1960–2007", *Journal of Research in Economics and International Finance*, Vol. 1, No. 5, pp. 141–149.

Anaman, K.A. (2006). "What Factors Have Influenced Economic Growth in Ghana?", *The Institute of Economic Affairs (IEA)*, Ghana Policy Analysis 2, Accra.

Baharumshah, A.Z. and S.W. Almasaied (2009). "Foreign Direct Investment and Economic Growth in Malaysia: Interactions with Human Capital and Financial Deepening", *Emerging Markets Finance and Trade*, Vol. 45, No. 1, pp. 90–102. doi:10.2753/ree1540-496x450106.

Dartey-Baah, Kwasi (2015). "Political Leadership in Ghana 1957 to 2010", *African Journal of Political Science and International Relations*, Vol. 9, No. 2, February, pp. 49–61.

Havi, Emmanuel K. Dodzi, Patrick Enu, F. Osei-Gyimah, Prudence Attah-Obeng and C.D.K. Opoku (2013). "Macroeconomic Determinants of Economic Growth in Ghana: Cointegration Approach", *European Scientific Journal*, Vol. 9, No. 19, July, ISSN 1857-7881, pp. 156–175.

Hussain, Zahid (2014). "Can Political Stability Hurt Economic Growth?", June, http://blogs.worldbank.org/endpovertyinsouthasia/can-political-stability-hurt-economic-growth Accessed 2/11/2019.

Navaratnam, Ramon V. (1997). *Managing the Malaysian Economy: Challenges and Prospects*, Selangor Darul Eshan, Malaysia, Pelanduk Publications.

Ofori, Daniel, Shadrach Ato-Mensah, Jinseng Zhu and Shadrach Ato-Mensah (2015). "Corruption, Foreign Direct Investment and Growth in Ghana: An Empirical Analysis", *European Journal of Business and Management*, Vol. 7, No. 23, ISSN 2222-1905 (Paper) ISSN 2222-2839 (Online), www.iiste.org Accessed 11/23/2019.

Index

Note: Page numbers in *italic* indicate a figure; page numbers in **bold** indicate a table on the corresponding page.

Printed in the United States
by Baker & Taylor Publisher Services